# LOVE, DAD

**Laurie Steed** is a writer, mentor, and manuscript assessor. His writing has been awarded, broadcast and published widely, including on BBC Radio 4 and in *Best Australian Stories* and *Award Winning Australian Writing*. He is the author of the novel *You Belong Here*, which was shortlisted for the Western Australian Premier's Book Awards, and has a PhD in Creative Writing from The University of Western Australia. He lives in Boorloo (Perth) with his wife and two sons.

# LOVE, DAD

## CONFESSIONS OF AN ANXIOUS FATHER

Laurie Steed

FREMANTLE PRESS

*For my wife and two beautiful boys*
*in love and gratitude*

# Contents

## SIGNIFICANT OTHERS



## HOLDING ON



## LETTING GO

# EXPECTING

This is not the book I set out to write.

I was going to write a memoir about a strong, resilient, and triumphant man and father – only doing that would have denied what it means to be an active, present parent. I could have said I was killing it, barely raising a sweat, but doing this would have enforced the idea that to be a man means you never have to say, 'I'm struggling'.

That tough, silent kind of manliness was sold hard to us as boys. When it came time for me to be a man, I thought 'sorted', because I already had my driver's licence, a car and a set of dumbbells. Soon enough, it was time to graduate from high school. I smeared Vegemite along the handrails on muck-up day, a rite of passage and inspired piece of petty vandalism to hide the fact that I was already lost before I'd walked that sloping driveway and out the gates that final time.

From then on, I worked mostly menial jobs, somehow successfully completed three degrees around those jobs, and during the fourth, became a father. I thought I'd built my warrior-self up perfectly in the preceding years. Instead, I had fashioned an approximation of what I thought a man was supposed to be; an 'Okay Laurie' to assuage fears, concerns, or panic on the back of becoming a dad.

*She'll be right. I mean, it can't be that hard, can it?*

It *can* be that hard. It can be really hard if things cascade, as if water were falling down around you. You go to take a breath but catch only a mouthful of water, barely knowing how this happened, or what, if anything, you can do to stop the flow.

Anxiety is a funny thing. It freaks you out, and then suddenly, and often without warning, the fear subsides. It comes back, of course, intensely sometimes, and yet I know that as a person living with anxiety, I can still be the best dad for my kids. I know that even in the midst of a storm, I'll find needed ways in which to connect with and validate their thoughts and feelings.

Working with my anxiety is like staring into the abyss. I'm now also committed to jumping into that chasm, to find out how it feels when I find a soft landing, or I'm caught by outstretched arms. It's deeply heartening to be held in such a space. I also know I won't always be caught, and so there's risk in writing these words. Still, I know that's where this starts for me; that in sharing my world there's the hope that others will relate to my story, and my intermittent feelings of 'not-enoughness'.

There are very few concrete truths about parenting that I can pass on without fear that they are at best simplistic, and at worst, grossly misleading. Instead, this book is the story of my slow (sometimes faltering) realisation that – as I continue on the life-changing and wondrous journey of parenthood – there is no right way to do any of this other than what works for me, and what frees me up to live a life in which I am my most authentic self.

I hope it helps you too.

# BIRTH

# It's Real, Love

I was born in Hamilton (Kirikiriroa), an inland city in the North Island of New Zealand (Aotearoa) and raised in a family of four kids. In my younger years, we spent most weekends in absurdly lush, cow-patted greenery, read *Footrot Flats* comics and argued whether 'One Step Ahead' was a better song than 'Dirty Creature'

I can't say I was the runt of the litter – I'm more stocky and a foot taller than any of them – however, I was the youngest. From early on, I was an epilogue to a family that already felt formed, on account of two older, more-established siblings, and then a third, who arrived soon after I was born.

Trent was adopted and brought into the family – and my bedroom – within the first three months of my life. Dad was a doctor at the time, doing the daily rounds at Waikato Hospital and had seen a boy on the wards. That boy, Trent, had been brought in because his mother was no longer able to care for him. My parents felt great empathy for the kid who at this stage had spent the first two and a half years of his life in hospital. Trent had health difficulties too, asthma and severe bronchitis, and the consensus was he wouldn't live past the age of three. Indeed, they would only let him be fostered with a doctor if he were to leave the hospital at all, such were his ongoing health concerns.

Mum and Dad made a decision that for however long Trent was around he would have a family to call his own. Looking back, I see how profoundly their generous decision to adopt my brother changed my own experience of childhood. As a brother, and a younger brother at that, I very much felt I existed alongside and in competition with Trent, and at times he received the attention I might otherwise have had, despite me at some point realising that the attention he'd received was mostly for the times he caused them concern rather than joy.

By 1986, when I was nine years old, my dad got a job opportunity in Perth, so the family moved from New Zealand to Australia, as my mum, dad, Luke and Eve had done a decade earlier when they moved from the United Kingdom to New Zealand.

That previous trip had led to some of the best years of their lives; this time around, Mum and Dad split up soon after our arrival in Western Australia.

There's not much to say about the divorce. Both Mum and Dad have talked to me about it, with each filling gaps in the other one's story. Watching it from the outside, it seemed at first strange, and then upsetting, and then just *done*. It felt a bit like looking at a building that was once a house but is now just a pile of bricks.

We got through it. I don't remember talking much about things with Luke and Eve but humour became the go-to for me and Trent. We created funny if unkind impressions of our parents' new partners to cope with just how much we missed the way things used to be.

Once we hit adolescence, we found unhelpful ways to deal with our hurt. Mine were less disruptive than Trent's, and I completed high school and immediately moved on to university. Trent dropped out of school and into a series of jobs, with those years dotted with time in prison and rehabilitation programs.

As I moved into adulthood, I realised I had taken on Mum and Dad's pact without thinking about it; that I, like them, would be there for my brother, sharing the load and the duty of care, even after the other siblings had all cut ties with their too-troubled brother.

I'd like to say being my brother's keeper never greatly affected me; by the time I hit my twenties, however, it was just another thing that was pulling me down. As therapy would soon show me, there was also more to discover.

I started going to counselling in 2002, just after my twenty-fifth birthday. I thought I was doing it to help my girlfriend, as she was due to go on antidepressants for the first time. It didn't take long, though, before we moved on to how I was travelling in my life and my relationships.

When I started therapy, I had no emotional literacy or self-awareness. Really, I sought psychology as an overweight person might seek a gym; it was a way to make the unmanageable more manageable, never really appreciating it might also greatly improve my mental health and give me a better outlook on life.

In the years leading up to 2007, when I met Annaya – my wife-to-be and herself a clinical psychologist – my counsellor and I discussed how certain key incidents, most notably how my parents' divorce and my friend Jeremy's suicide when I was nineteen, had shaped my view of the world.

No one had helped me grieve the death of my friend. My mates didn't check in much in the aftermath, and I'll admit, I didn't check in much on them either. No pamphlets arrived, and no people came up, and said, 'Hey, mate, I hear you lost your friend. Are you okay?'

With that in mind, those conversations with my counsellor were immensely liberating. I'd not known how much my friend's death had turned me into a loner, how I'd presumed no one would ever understand my trauma, and how very afraid I was of loving someone as much as I had loved Jeremy.

We didn't talk too much about those years before things came to a head, when I was out of home at seventeen, moving from place to place, searching for something that felt stable and supportive, but mostly hamstrung by my friendship group being a roving three-man party forever looking for a place to kick-off, carry on or crash for the night. In the years after Jeremy died, I first spent time living in Scotland, and then, once back in Australia, began my first long-term relationships, which fell apart predominantly because I did not yet feel safe to be so reliant on another human being.

I eventually made inroads in this area with my psychologist and in time was ready to start a new relationship. Once I met Annaya, and after she had moved to Melbourne from Perth, I began working with a new psychologist. Almost immediately, Daniel could spot when I was genuinely sharing and when

I was performing, deflecting or people-pleasing. We trod water for a while: my thoughts, opinions and background, and then in time we moved on to my parents and their divorce.

'It doesn't affect you?'

'Not really. It was a long time ago. And anyway, they didn't love each other.'

'You really believe that?'

'They would have stayed together. They could have made it work if they had cared enough to do it.'

He paused, waiting.

'Don't,' I said.

'What?'

'I'm serious, don't do that. I know what you're doing.'

Again, he paused. 'What am I doing?'

'Can we not talk about this anymore?'

'Okay. Perhaps we'll come back to it.'

Things went on like this for months, with me engaged to Annaya – sharing coffees, movies and dinner dates on the streets of Camberwell, in Melbourne's east – while inside I felt the fear take over, telling me it would be better if I walked away.

And then one day, my fears seemed to have won. I walked into my psychologist's office. I told him my marriage wasn't going to work, the same way none of my relationships had worked. The way my mum and dad were never going to work.

'Never? They worked for seventeen years, and four kids, right?'

I paused. 'They said they loved each other.'

'They did,' said Daniel.

'Then why did they split up?'

He turned the question back on me. 'You know, don't you. You just don't want to admit it.'

'I don't.'

'Yes, you do. You know why.' He paused. 'It just happened because sometimes, things just happen, and all the thinking in the world won't put your family back together.' He watched me for a while, irritated. 'So you're going to quit?'

I nodded.

'See, here's the thing,' he said. 'If you give up, the way your parents "gave up", and the way you gave up those other times, then it wins. Not the fear, or your anxiety. But the pain, and all that suffering. You let it win because you're not willing to take the risk.'

He waited. Passed me a box of tissues and waited some more. Not happy or particularly impressed with his realisation, but aware that I needed to be challenged before it was too late.

In December 2010, Annaya and I fly back to Boorloo (Perth) for our wedding, staying at her parents' house. It's an anxious trip and not just because we're getting married. As with my dad, who suffered his first heart attack in 2005, Annaya's father has been in and out of hospital with heart problems in the years prior. The related anxiety in coping with her father's fragility is taking its toll on Annaya, especially because we are living on the other side of the country.

I have my own strained relationship with Boorloo. It's not so much the city that's the problem. It's more that my parents split up the moment we arrived. Their divorce and its subsequent fallout were simultaneously both a distressingly abrupt ending and one hell of an opening chapter. So, it's not all that surprising when, I turn to Annaya, having made it back to Perth, and say, 'I know, it's great to be back home and all, but if we end up living here, please shoot me.'

'It will pass,' says Annaya in her most soothing clin-psych voice.

*It will come back*, I think, *because it always does.*

On the day before my wedding, I drive to my father's house in York, Western Australia, a wheatbelt town where the powerlines drape from house to house and bark hangs off trees, dangling and dancing in the wind. My brother Trent's there too. Sharing this moment with the two of them feels like a particularly big deal. Marriage to me had always been a pipedream, and yet we're here on the precipice of the one day I could never fully picture.

Even so, it's not until we're driving to the wedding venue, playing 'You've Got the Love' by Florence + the Machine, that it hits me – that this time, I've conquered the mountain.

We reach the accommodation, a sleepy resort away in the Swan Valley, get dressed, and then it's time to drive over to the wedding venue. From there I have some nervous conversations with friends and family, as I wait for my soon-to-be wife to arrive.

Once the music begins and she walks into view, I see only Annaya. She's dressed in white, olive skin, petite, angelic and smiling back at me. Through the readings and our vows,

I can't look away, and in that moment, all my worries and fears disappear.

My vows are wordy, awkward. I am trying to say *I trust you and I love you and I cannot believe that I am here with you, now, and I will always be with you from this moment on.*

Holding her hand, as we lead into the 'I do', I see all I've ever done was leading me to her. That I'd been waiting for her. That I was terrified she would never come. That thirty years is but a blip once your true love arrives. That I would live another life just for her to kiss me, hold me close and say, 'I love you.'

And so we dance our bridal waltz to 'Real Love' by Regina Spektor. And on it stretches, that first night, and I don't know if I have touched a person's face or hand so often in the course of an evening to be sure that she, and this, is real.

Soon after we're married, my internal narrative changes from *Mate, don't mess this up* to *I think, if I open up and continue to talk with her then we are going to be okay*. It's the first time in my life I've had this thought. In my earlier relationships, the message so often seemed to be *It's just a shame that this could never work out.*

With Annaya, a couple of challenges led to greater connection between us. Being in a long-distance relationship for a year and a half meant talking a lot, and more importantly, missing each other like crazy. I remember the Skype calls from those first two years, wanting only to reach through the screen to be able to touch her. Those video calls gave us tiny moments of respite, whether it was making her laugh, or us sharing a tough time, until the day she came to Melbourne to live while I completed my degree.

Which is not to say *life* became easier after that. It's more that for the first time in any of my relationships, we had two people on the same team. In the past, either me or my partner had issues that slowed us or otherwise got in the way of clear communication. In Annaya's eyes, I saw none of that. We had both travelled through various life challenges, were introduced to each other by a mutual friend with a huge heart and a way of knowing things one can't otherwise possibly know. Working outside of logic or grand plans, she simply put us in the same place to see what might happen. And in time, we made a life, and found much love on the leaf-strewn streets of Melbourne's inner suburbs.

And then, with my Master of Editing and Publishing completed, it was time to return to Perth, only this time with Annaya – two people in no hurry to leave the relationship or in any way shirk our duty to us, and to our future.

I move into her flat in a gated apartment complex in Joondalup, a satellite city of Perth. With our boxes hauled up two flights of stairs and our furniture in place, I wonder if I might be *that* kind of man after all: one more willing to let go of the past, to build a future, and no longer so scared of stepping into the unknown.

I start my PhD in Creative Writing later that year. I am quietly confident that the book I'm writing will be the making of me. I've also made a concrete decision to solely prioritise my writing throughout these next three years. It's a promise to myself of sorts; a reward for those hard years working low-level jobs while in pursuit of a literary career.

Still, none of matters when halfway into that PhD, Annaya wakes me up, mid-nap.

She's holding a test and, judging from the lines on its indicator, we have passed with flying colours.

# Disquiet

In the space of three days, I go from chill to nervous about the forthcoming addition to our family. Why am I so terrified? Well, for starters, everything I know about babies I learned while 'reading' Peter Mayle's illustrated book for kids, *Where Did I Come From?*, when I was seven years old.

A lot went over my head. I do remember, though, precisely when we read it: Dad was at work, and Mum had gone out somewhere with Eve, leaving Luke in charge. That worked for about two minutes until Trent found the book on the shelf, and this somehow ended with us first finding and then putting on condoms on our flaccid willies, wiggling them around and shouting, 'We're going to make a baby!'

We learned very little that day. Even now, while halfway through my PhD studies and with a bub fast growing, I know little more.

I see a Perth-based psychologist, Elliot, quite frequently in this period. Like Daniel, his office is in one of the city's more wealthy suburbs, but unlike Daniel, Elliot is soon to retire and so our conversations have a more patient, curious feel than the necessarily interrogative approach of Daniel in the lead-up to my wedding. I tell him a bit about my PhD and the baby on the way, and eventually he suggests anti-anxiety medication, at least for those early months.

I ask, 'Are there any side effects?'

He says, 'Yes, of course, there are always side effects, but there are many more from having not taken them if you're about to have a baby.'

I say, 'Does everyone freak out at this point?'

'Not everyone,' says Elliot, 'but for those that do, there's no shame in getting something to help during what's likely to be a stressful time.'

I work long days in 'The Cave' as if I might complete my PhD, just in time, when really, I have at least another eighteen months to go. I hope to come back to it at some point, although I have no idea how things will look after the baby shows up.

The Cave is so named, incidentally, because of its absence of natural light. It's nestled away in the arts precinct of my university at the top of a flight of stairs. I share the space with a bunch of anthropology PhD students. My desk faces the wall, not my choice, although I support its cocoon-like feel. I likely would have never ventured out from behind it at all were it not for one day when a woman came over, extended her hand, and said, 'My name's Michelle. I'm doing a PhD in Creative Writing. What are you studying?' and I just about jumped up and hugged her right there.

My Creative Writing PhD project is made up of two parts. The first, my creative component, is *You Belong Here*, an ambivalent family love story told from the point of view of each of the five family members. My critical component, 'Autobiography and Masculinity in *You Belong Here*' uses Western Australian authors Tim Winton and Kim Scott as a departure point for a continued exploration of the more self-aware, emotionally literate male characters who appear in my fiction.

Since starting in earnest, it's been nice to have Michelle – though at some point, her name is shortened, as is mine, and things quickly became the Mish and Loz show – working alongside me in our dimly lit bunker. We still mostly write in silence, or with headphones in, but over time that extends to coffees down at Reid Library and discussions about books and our writing.

Mish is sharp, funny and self-deprecating, and I hope one day her book is out so I can shout its merits to the world. At present, neither of us are particularly well known as WA writers, although we both work hard, and if we wrote novels rather than short stories, we'd be more well-known than we currently are.

Back home, Annaya throws up quite a bit, most often on her way to the car in the morning. We're still so in love that I think it's cute. She thinks it's gross, and inconvenient, and that I am a total weirdo.

We buy socks so small they fit on my fingers. We buy mittens, like they'll ever be used. My friend Zig, not a dad, but an uncle of note, posts us a pack of bibs from Melbourne with a note that reads, 'You'll need these.'

*For meals?* I text back in my thank-you message.

No, he replies, and leaves it at that.

Annaya's morning sickness dissipates and the existential

crisis kicks in; my research turns to all things birth-related. I read serious books like *What to Expect When You're Expecting* by Heidi Murkoff. I read funny books like Kaz Cooke's *Up the Duff*, because while I don't yet know what parenting will be like, I get the feeling I am going to need a sense of humour.

We watch *Three Men and a Baby* but I can't work out which doofus I'm supposed to be out of Ted Danson, Tom Selleck and Steve Guttenberg. I watch the episode of *Friends* where Rachel has the baby and decide I do *not* want Ross present at the birth.

We go to our nineteen-week ultrasound and there is now a tiny thing inside, the ultrasound providing a bird's-eye view into my partner's tummy.

'You're having a boy,' the nurse says.

I take Annaya's hand. 'Are you happy?'

She nods. 'You think we'll be good parents?'

'I don't know,' I say, but I hope that we will.

There are many more appointments and it's clear the nurses and obstetricians are taking notes about something, though I've no clue what that is. For the most part, we just sit there, as if we've been cast for a TV show but we don't yet know what the show is.

There is something adorable about Annaya throughout this stage. She waddles, rather than walks. It's winter, so she's perpetually in hats and beanies. At one point of many, I take a photo: she's holding two tiny baby socks upon her bulging baby belly, and I can't take it, the cuteness overload is too much, and it's hard to believe I'm living my life and not recounting scenes from a Richard Curtis film.

She rests a lot. I try and sometimes fail to do the housework – certain items of clothing need protection from each other, apparently, and so must be kept protected in thin, zippable bags. Dejected, I retreat to the kitchen. I worked in cafes and restaurants as a cook when I was younger, so I'm a beast when it comes to baking. Muffins, pastries, you name it; for me, it's not so much about the delicate interplay between butter, flour and baking powder as it is about finding ways to hit the yum button for my friends and family.

More generally, I worry about all kinds of things. When to introduce my kid to the wonders of *The Neverending Story*? What if he likes Christina Aguilera more than Britney Spears? What do babies eat? Do you carry a bub like luggage, or like a vase?

At that point, I wonder how does *anything* work? And again have no clue. Somehow, despite a life of nearly thirty-six years, my breadth of knowledge is restricted mostly to yacht rock, eighties films and the NBA.

Annaya grows bigger. She's a goddess, a cherub. She's tired, tiny and patient most days. She rocks a baby-belly, obligingly posing for pregnancy pics, the first photos of her and our baby together, although as yet, we've not named him.

In time, Annaya finishes work, and takes up on the living room couch. I let her be, and hide out in the home office most days – I'm starting to fret and I don't want her or the baby to feel that. Time compacts in this period, as I try to balance dedicated work on my PhD with prep for the baby. Eventually, his room is complete, his cot fully assembled, with stick-on giraffes across the wall, a mobile dancing in the light gusts of the air-conditioning, and a handful of plush dinosaurs and koala teddies bunched up in the corner.

I wonder how to slow time. I think, is there someone you can hire who just says, 'Wait, this is how you do it, from birth to school to graduation?'

So many things to do, with so little time.

Mum says she had the opposite problem, and eventually took matters into her own hands when she was pregnant with me, and I was past my due date. So, one Tuesday, she went to a kindy lunch, came home. Then she got up on a chair and jumped to the ground to speed things up. It turns out that did the job; she rang my dad to come pick her up and I was born later that afternoon.

That's one thing we have in our favour: I'm working from home for the final weeks of the pregnancy in case we need to head into the hospital at any point, and when I'm not home, Annaya can call or text me. And, while I've not always been the biggest fan of mobile phones, they play a vital part in our pregnancy, from texts coordinating appointments to charting our baby's growth with the *Sprout Baby* app.

It's hard to get my head around those experiential differences between my parents having me, and me and Annaya on our way to the birth of our first child. Just as the older generation will always struggle to understand the realities of the younger generation, the reverse also seemingly applies. The rituals, from births to deaths to marriages, are anchored as part of life. The specifics will vary so greatly from generation to generation, though, that any wisdom found and shared is more like a bone than the full skeleton.

We argue about the name. She suggests Leo, I say he's a boy, not a cereal mascot, and what about Noah, how's the narrative arc on that? She makes a face and we agree to disagree. I buy her blocks of Lindt, a massage in a place with fresh flowers, pastel colours and loose-leaf tea. I hope they are gentle and kind to Annaya and our baby, hands cupped super soft as they work their way around the bump.

As we prepare for the real deal, I continue to work on my PhD, with my novel, *You Belong Here*, just warming up, and the critical component, my exegesis, admittedly a complete shambles.

Ever closer to the due date, marking off the calendar with crosses. Late night calls with my mum, with the pretence of some trivial question, but really to talk to someone who's done this before.

'You nervous?'

'No,' I lie.

'There is *nothing* like what you are about to go through,' she says, and I wonder what she means.

I'm edging towards a state of full-blown panic by this point. I take trips to Baby Bunting (which is like a Kmart for expectant parents) and Ikea (which is like hell for everyone). I drive to Bunnings to get WD-40 in case something squeaks or is otherwise in need of lubrication.

I ring my friend, Dash. He is my oldest friend from high school. He's originally from Pennsylvania, loves hoops and hip-hop, and is wicked smart, if admittedly a bit of a hater sometimes. On a good day, though, he feels profoundly connected to my soul: a thoughtful, empathetic and funny-as-hell friend with whom I can talk through anything.

He says he has a Kombi van now, and it's sick. 'You should hear T-Pain on that stereo, and there's no way the Heat are going to win the NBA championship again next year, get real, it's Sixers' time, fool. All that baby-daddy juice, it's playing with your brain, you know?'

Oh, I know, and in the coming weeks, my anxiety continues to grow. What if there's a storm? How many nappies are too many? How much sleep do you legally need to be able to drive a car? Will I be able to keep up with *Veep*? What on earth shall we call this baby? Can you fail a prenatal workshop, and if you do, does that mean you can't have the baby?

We return to Baby Bunting, pacing the aisles like doomsday preppers. We buy soft cushions in the shapes of moons, and wall-art of balloons and clumsy zebras, and I'm pretty sure there's Winnie the Pooh in there somewhere, as there always is.

Overwhelmed, I listen to 'Father and Son' by Cat Stevens and tear up at the bit when he tries to explain things to his young, errant son.

I ring my dad. Tell him I'm freaking out. He comes back less Cat Stevens and more Bertrand Russell.

'Well,' he says, 'you see, the thing about having children is you'll barely talk to them for the first five years of their life.'

'But you talked to me.'

'I don't mean with you and I,' he says, backtracking. 'In general. Rushes by. You'll hardly even know you're a parent.'

As we're talking, I look across at Annaya. She smiles at me, hopeful and herself a little anxious. Even then, I get the feeling things will be vastly different for us, and that from the time the baby arrives, and for the rest of our lives, we will very much know we are parents.

I don't call Dad as much after that. Nor do I call my brother Luke, for reasons I can't fully articulate, though he is also a dad. I mean he has enough to worry about with his own kids. I figure this is my mess, or my gift, or *something* – right now it's hard to tell exactly what we've found in the lead-up to becoming new parents.

In Noah's birth, I also see an opportunity to learn more about my father, and how life was for him at that same stage. I picture afternoons on the balcony spent discussing approaches to parenting. Memories he had of us when we were little. Memories of his dad if he has any, although I know his father was a little more distant than most, and not like mine, into whose lap I climbed most nights if he was home from the hospital in time.

I make up a list of questions to ask my father. A series of topics to address: nappy bags vs nappy bins, and the classic bicarbonate soda debate, as it relates to nappy pong. Cloth versus disposable nappies. Washing poo off said cloth nappies versus using a fire hose to spray it off. How to get by on little to no sleep. What to say to yourself when your baby is screaming so loud it's breaking glassware.

Most nights, I retreat to a lounge chair, and read another parenting book. I put up another piece of wall art. Many nights, I walk into the spare room, previously filled with a double bed, but which now contains a cot.

'Come to bed,' says Annaya from the doorway.

'In a bit.'

But I don't come for quite a while. I tell this boy, not yet arrived, that I'm going to be a good dad. That I'll do everything I can to ensure he's safe, happy and healthy.

I tell him that one time I made a 'hairy harry' at primary school, this ball of dirt and seeds inside a tied-up pair of pantyhose, with googly eyes on the outside. I say that over time, that ball of dirt grew green hair up top – a teenage plant, with sass, vigour and charm.

I admit this analogy is not at all appropriate; that the stakes are a little higher in this instance, hence the fretting, promising and the distinct lack of a glass jar or googly eyes. Because this time I am not raising a plant, I'll be raising a boy. As in, I will be his dad, which is a thought so big, and so ridiculous I can barely get my head around it.

# After The Fall

Annaya and I walk down to the local café on a Saturday morning. It's coming into Djilba, a sunny early August day in Joondalup, a satellite city thirty minutes north of Perth.

In our last childless days on Wattlebird Loop, we watch films that are most definitely not about having babies. We sit on the balcony in the afternoons if the weather permits, looking out through trees and on to Lake Joondalup. Most mornings we wake late, cuddle through from eight until ten, and get up only for our morning coffee, or to lazily make our way through brunch.

It's a franchise cafe, but the owner, Khalil, keeps things personal. He's strong and tanned, looking something like a cross between Jason Statham and actor and former model Boris Kodjoe. He's always happy to see us, knows us by name, and it feels as though under the surface he's a man of quiet strength, resilience and compassion.

Khalil takes our breakfast order at the counter, makes some polite chat and we head to a table, grabbing two copies of Saturday's *West Weekend* along the way.

Being a chain, the coffees come quick – fewer matchas, soys or dirty chais – and soon enough, our meals are there too, a full veggie brekky for me, and bacon and eggs for Annaya.

Halfway through our meals, my phone rings. I pick it up. It's Alice, my dad's third wife.

'Hey, Alice.'

'Hi, Laurie,' she says, a shake in her voice, and then she pauses. 'You'd better sit down.'

I *am* sitting down, so from that point, we're screwed. 'What's going on?'

'There's been an accident,' she says. 'Your father is in an ambulance. He's on the way to hospital.'

'What kind of accident?'

'He fell off the roof,' she says. I wait for her to continue, but she doesn't, and instead, she starts to cry.

I say I'll head straight to Northam but she says they'll most likely take him to Royal Perth Hospital and operate on him from there.

And so, we go from drinking coffee in a cafe, on a call talking about my dad's accident, to me baking scrolls, scones and muffins. They're really good muffins – I could make muffins in a dust storm – but it's weird, and I mean really weird, to be so feverishly cooking things to stop from thinking about Dad.

I apply the right measurements of buttermilk to create an optimal fluffiness in the muffin. I think about Dad's cheesy, seeded mustard grills he'd bring out while we watched TV together. I think about baking scrolls – and then I am baking scrolls. All the time getting updates from Alice, yet nothing is conclusive.

Then finally, after hours of manic baking – from flour to bowl to pastry to oven to dishes, and then the same all over again – and then it's time to head to Royal Perth Hospital with Annaya and my older brother, Luke.

Luke was, and still is, a heavy metal musician, although his genre of choice is now closer to horror metal. What's horror metal? It's as it sounds, and my brother plays it well. Slow, sparse, haunting instrumentation. In the videos, he cuts together kaleidoscopic horror-scapes of stock footage – think the slicing of the cow's eye in Buñuel's *Un Chien Andalou* or the fever dreams of early animation, and you're on the right track.

We don't listen to his music or any other music, though, because there is no music suitable for when you're headed to see your father in the intensive care unit.

We arrive at the ICU and the doctors and Alice bring us up to speed.

Dad fell off the roof while cleaning a gutter and cracked his head open. Alice had been at work when he fell. The dogs, all four of them, saw him fall and began barking. That was how she found out. Her neighbours, put out by the noise, called her to come home and shut the dogs up, not knowing they were barking to alert someone, as Dad lay unconscious and bleeding on the concrete.

They need someone to sign off drilling into his skull to relieve the pressure. Luke nods to me as if to say, 'All yours.' As I sign, I hear my father's voice in my head, saying, *Who's the bright spark who just signed off on drilling into my head?*

I think, *It's me, Dad, it's Laurie, and I promise, we are going to get you out of here.*

The next day, my other brother, Trent, and my sister, Eve, arrive, and the rest of us head back to hospital. We're crammed into this tiny ICU waiting room. Alice watches tribal music videos on her iPad, with the volume up high. Luke's using his mini tablet as a phone, so he looks like an eighties businessman. Trent's jumpy, as he's not on the best of terms with anyone other than me, and Eve's sharing the news with Dad's relatives in England. That's partly as it's earlier in the day there, but just as much because Alice is particularly shaken up by Dad's fall and in no state to be talking to the family.

Eventually Annaya retires from hospital visits – she's damn near ready to pop – and in the following days, it's the five of us, in and out of ICU, perpetually tired. Trent's bunking down at mine, Luke at his place, and Eve, who lives down south, stays with a friend.

'We're going to get you out of here,' I say, again and again to my comatose father, to the point that it eventually it becomes my mantra.

We are allowed to visit his ICU bed in twos – this usually means Eve and Luke as one pair, Alice on her own, and me and Trent as the last pair in the group. Luke is glued to his phone, and Trent's starting to look like he could do with some chemical enhancement.

Each morning starts to feel the same. To get us through the trip to the hospital, Trent and I find a song, 'Pompeii' by Bastille, that we listen to each morning. The bass thumps the inside of my Elantra as we drive into the city. Trent pats his leg, nervous, until one time I punch his arm, and he nods and stops.

Eve and Alice sit there in that tiny ICU waiting room day after day, holding each other's hand. I want to tell them, 'It's okay, I've done this before, and you should never listen to a doctor on the first day because they're guessing almost as much as you are.'

I don't tell them that fifteen years earlier, my friend fell twenty metres off a rope, and into a hospital bed. I skip over us sitting by his bedside day after day, until one day he finally woke, and I am not a religious man, but on that day, I came close, and I felt my friend's calloused hand, tears streaming down my face as we gazed back at each other.

In the early days of my father's coma, we're told he's going to die, and that he might be brain-dead; I bake a shitload of stuff, from crêpes through to scones and *pain au chocolat*. The days at the hospital are long, although we see Dad move sometimes, and hope, or maybe wish that it might mean something.

And then one day, Eve comes in from being bedside, tears rolling down her cheeks. She says, 'He's up: Dad's awake,' and we take turns going in to see him. I can't stop smiling, this time holding his much thinner hand, but the smile is there, and it seems we dodged a bullet.

Within a few days, it's clear he's not full-strength. On a visit soon after he wakes, he sits me down and briefs me about the construction of a hospital in Northam. He mentions my role and the need to employ various contractors to ensure the job gets done. He then thanks me for the meeting and asks if I can open the main door. I go to do this when a matron calls out,

'Not so fast, Dr Steed,' and rushes to stop me.

Another time, I sit down with my dad, and he takes my hand, and says, 'Hello, darling.' A younger nurse comes over, briefs him on where he's at, and recent test results, and he nods as if thoroughly considering the new information, before saying, 'Are you going to give Laurie your phone number?' She laughs, and moves on to talk of trauma in the brain, of the importance of familiar faces and the need for prolonged rehabilitation. He nods again, seemingly more confused this time, turns to me, and says, 'Laurie, are you going to get this girl's phone number?'

I say, 'No, Dad,' because I have a wife at home. And a baby on the way. And a new life, quickly picking up speed.

Beneath the fear and the grief, I'm frustrated by Dad dropping out at such a pivotal time. I think about that a lot, gearing up to be a dad with mine out of action. Seeking solace and guidance, but instead, playing word-salad with Dad's brain, still recovering from trauma.

The night in which my father is granted release to move into a rehabilitation program, I come home exhausted. It's been two weeks since the accident. I go through the latest developments with Annaya. She says, 'Wow, you're being so strong about all of this.'

I want to tell her I'm not. That I'm drowning. That I don't know how to do this. That I thought someone would help me with this.

She takes me to bed, holds me till my heart rate slows, and I drift into a fitful, frantic sleep.

## Passenger

It's four thirty am, too early in anyone's language. I wake to my hand being squeezed in a vice, and Annaya screams, 'It hurts! It hurts!'

I say, 'What time is it?' Her eyes bulge, and she says, 'It's hurting me.'

I say, 'Oh, honey,' understanding there's clearly some sense of unrest.

She squeezes my hand.

I say, 'Can you describe the pain?' and it looks like she's going to kill me with something, maybe the alarm clock, but then she squeezes some more and cries, and I say, 'Oh, wow, is it time to have the baby?'

It's not time to have the baby. I ring the hospital, and they tell us to stay home, as things are only just beginning. As dawn arises and the day begins, I make myself useful. I split open a raspberry and white choc scone and eat both parts. I give Annaya a tub of Connoisseur ice-cream with a teaspoon in it. She doesn't drink coffee or Coke, so I make her tea, which is kind of like waving a wet wipe at a fire, but we carry on regardless, her squeezing my hand and me saying, 'Angel,' until she grips my hand again and tells me to again ring the hospital.

They tell us to stay home, as things are still just getting started.

We stay home and watch this awful movie. I mean, seriously, it's the pits. I'm watching it, and I keep thinking, why does this movie hurt my hand so much? Then I realise it's Annaya, she's squeezing my fingers while doing this locomotive breathing thing, thighs akimbo and calves against each other, so she's formed an X, a giant cross on the day, and this D+ film we're watching.

At six pm that night, we finally head into the hospital. It's raining. There are no parking spots so I take those one of those ones you always get a ticket for parking too long in, and think, *I'll move it later.*

There's no one in the lobby aside from the receptionist, no staff this side of the Swan River it seems, but boy does it look nice.

We take the lift and make our way to the maternity ward. My hand is crushed by this point, and Annaya has gone full locomotive with the huffing and puffing. After months of planning, round after round of consultation, our obstetrician's not available on the night. I freak. But then her backup arrives, and she's cool and calm. She walks in with a takeaway coffee at seven pm on a Saturday night, and immediately, I like her. It's time now, our time, with Annaya on the cusp of giving birth, and I don't know what it is I should be doing, so I keep saying, 'It's okay,' over and over, as if thinking this might make it so.

At that point, a nurse levels a horse syringe towards Annaya's back. Annaya says she wants the drugs – and I can't blame her, I want the drugs too. But apparently, I'm not allowed to have the drugs because I'm 'not pregnant'. So, they give Annaya the drugs, and they pass me a set of scrubs that wouldn't fit a child, let alone a man.

I go to the bathroom, and in there I stretch out quickly, first left then right but to no effect, and when the scrubs are finally on, the zip goes to just above my belly button. My package, which isn't the size of an elephant's trunk, looks positively obscene against such tight-fitting maroon cotton; and as for my bum, well, let's say I ride the seam horse all the way to the operating room.

I turn to Annaya, and say, 'This looks ridiculous! It's way too tight.' She takes a hit of the oxygen, as the epidural has not yet kicked in, smiles, and says, 'You're *cute*.'

I go to move the car, heading out to long-term parking, as cotton-ball clouds of grey on a dark sky begin to gather, the beginnings of a storm. By the time I get back, our obstetrician says there's meconium in the womb and there's a risk that our boy has swallowed some in transit. She wonders aloud why we didn't come in earlier, and I wonder that too – and pretty angrily at that – but that feeling passes because she says we need to go to the operating room, right now, for an emergency C-section.

I'd heard the term 'C-section' before – my sister opted to have one when she had her first child. People opt for planned caesareans all the time and more power to them. Emergency C-sections, though, are not something you choose. They're complicated and quite frightening in that the mother, the baby, or both, are at significant risk, so the baby needs to come out *now*.

A nurse tells me two out of every five caesareans are unplanned or emergency procedures. While I take solace that they're necessarily familiar to medical professionals, I hope you, the reader, never have to go through one. Or if you do, that things turn out okay in the end, and you think, *I'm so glad my baby's okay, and my love, she's okay too, and oh shit, oh shit, we really just went through that, didn't we?*

But that comes later. Right now, they're working behind a sheet to separate us from the cutting, and it's the most horrendous shadow play of all time, and it's endless, really endless. Annaya is losing consciousness. I'm thinking, *Please, be okay*, and then there's a sound I've never heard before. It's like a cry but more a steady, buzzing sob, with a hiccup or two in the mix, and I think, *My God, it's him. That's my son, he's here.*

I go across, say, 'Hey, little man,' and he's tiny and covered in gunk, looking like he's been splattered by the inside of a tissue. And then we cut the cord, and even as it's happening, amid all that chaos, another thought takes its place, and I think, *Oh my God, I love you so, so much.*

Annaya's out after that (I mean fair enough, she just had major surgery) and they take our son to the neonatal intensive care unit. Annaya made it through okay (I know because I saw her smile, eyes closed when they took the pic with us holding the baby), but our little man's still in trouble, and so the first thing they have to do is suck out the meconium.

It feels strange with everyone asleep but me. I mean, I don't know that my baby's asleep, but they whisked him away straight after. I miss him already – he had this squishy, Churchill face, and he rocked a tiny beanie like a champ. I wonder what else I'm supposed to do with my life from now on, other than look after him.

I watch Annaya in quiet awe as she sleeps. My wife. Our boy's mum. A goddess.

I touch her cheek, but she doesn't stir. That's okay. While I feel triggered at that point – for I often feel triggered when I am suddenly on my own and unable to find another person with whom to talk things through, or to share my emotions – I'm also not sure what I would say if she was awake, or how I'd unpack all we just went through.

The paediatrician comes in with two nurses, shakes my hand like I've taken on a mortgage. He sees Annaya sleeping, nods to himself. Then he turns to me, his decision made, and tells me I'm doing the first skin-on-skin and the first feed.

I say, 'Are you sure?' and he looks at me as though I've cheated on a test.

'We're sure,' he says. 'Head on up and they'll tell you what to do.'

## Reborn

Everything inside the neonatal ward is tiny, from elevated cots with heat lamps to tiny bubs – their cots like cars in a carpark – all beanied-up, with some crying, and some sleeping.

I find my boy under the heat lamp, in a tiny nappy and sky-blue beanie so small it would fit in the palm of my hand. I put out my little finger and he grasps it, holds it tight, first contact on this stormy Saturday night.

A nurse gives me a milk bottle, tells me it's warm but then reminds me to always check the temperature by squirting a little out onto the back of my hand. Slowly, he sucks out his first feed, his palm latched onto the little finger of my right, non-feeding hand. When that's done, a nurse holds him while I unbutton my shirt.

The blanket has warmed up his body but his hands are still freezing, so I lift him up and cradle him close to my chest, our first skin-on-skin. He's nestled in snugly; even so, I'm wary of keeping him away from the heat lamp for too long. I sneak a sniff of his downy scalp. I whisper, 'I love you, Junior.'

He nudges into me, his eyes barely open, tiny and fragile. It's huge and incredibly to see my future cradled in my arms. Yet at the same I feel something just as profound.

*I'm now a dad, and still I've not yet worked out how to be a man.*

When I get back to the room I say, 'We need to give him a name.'

'What do you think?' says Annaya.

'I think you gave birth to a living, breathing baby boy,' I say, 'And that we nearly lost him before we'd even started. You get to call him what you want.'

'Noah,' she says.

'I thought you wanted to call him Leo.'

'He's not a Leo, he's Noah,' she says, and that is that.

It's another twenty-four hours before our boy is brought to us, though only for a visit. In the meantime, I ferry Annaya up in a wheelchair. She's on oxycodone and is noddy as all hell, but you try to be Kate Middleton a day after an emergency caesarean section.

On my second visit that day, there's a West Coast Eagles tumbler waiting for me. There's a card too, red, with Junior's tiny footprints stamped on it in blue and, the words 'Happy Father's Day.'

Two days after the birth, they bring our son to the ward, this time for good.

Annaya is still exhausted and can barely move. It's eight pm when they bring him down. Annaya gives him a feed, puts him to bed and at around ten pm he wakes again. We page the nurse. She rushes in, says, 'It's okay, I'm here, it's alright.' She taps Annaya on the shoulder, says, 'Go to bed, my darling,' scoops the baby with one hand, and then signs *come here* to me with her index finger. I follow as she walks me out of the room, down the hallway, turning down another hallway, all the way to the end, until we're at the tearoom. She lets me in, smiles, and says, 'Good luck,' as she closes the door.

'Wait.'

'He's just a bit startled,' she says. 'Sometimes they sleep, and sometimes they don't.'

He continues to cry, so I rock him, and soothe him. I say I soothe him, really, it's more the calm voice you'd use when you've come across a bear but don't want it to attack you. He keeps crying so I adjust my approach. I sing the chorus from East 17's 'It's Alright' at an engaged, excited pace. I sing 'Everything's Alright' from *Jesus Christ Superstar* the way Kate Ceberano would sing it at, say, a gala performance. And then, as I sing 'No Woman, No Cry', I stretch to try to catch the sweet, soulful spirit of Bob Marley, who was also a dad – although he wrote songs that touched the globe, and I'm a dude in a tearoom wearing trackies and a hoodie, doing anything I can to stop my boy from crying.

Eventually, it works. He calms, and then stares up at me, opal eyes transfixed on this big, sprawling, singing buffoon.

The moment lasts for quite a while. Nothing to do, just someone to be, for as long as I'm needed.

The days after the birth are heightened. Annaya's parents and her brother visit a couple of times. My own live far away. It's three weeks since Dad was admitted into hospital and placed in an induced coma, and one since he was sent to the Shenton

Park Hospital rehabilitation facility. My mother and sister live down in the south-west of Western Australia, around five hours drive from Perth.

It's tough not having them around at the birth, although I imagine it was equally tough for my elder brother, Luke, all those years ago, alone in a cold, clinical hospital, welcoming his new family without the company of those from his old family. Perhaps it's karma, too – I'd been living with my sister down south, before I followed a girl across Australia only weeks before my sister was due to give birth. And, while said sister had played a part in that departure, I imagine it was also challenging for her, to have had me spend so much time with her during the pregnancy, but not be at the birth.

So, I'm heightened, moved to tears by a woman who pours me milk for my tea, infuriated by a nurse not yet attending to the call button. Every now and then, I'll meet another mum or dad in the tearoom, a shared, nervous smile as we cocoon our arrivals from the sound, the light and the world.

For the most part, we stare into the eyes of our babies, hopeful, frozen – suspended in the newness of it all.

For the rest of our stay, we play at being parents while being in a place with no phones, no neighbours and a nurse we can call at a heartbeat. It's a holding pattern of sorts. The room is small, the baby quite literally the focus of the room. As the days progress, we take turns looking after this tiny question mark that sits in our arms, wondering who will come to rescue us.

I take a ridiculous number of photos, most of him looking

mildly irked, slightly confused or a little unwell. I look happy but tired. Annaya glows, radiating warmth, and I am blown away by how close I feel to her.

I ask the nurses, 'Can we stay?' and I don't mean in the hospital. I mean in this time, with this level of hope, faith and wonder.

We leave the hospital after seven days of wake-ups, check-ups and cups of tea. We are not relieved or at all excited. We are terrified of the people around us, first outside the maternity ward, and then again downstairs in the hospital lobby. It's raining hard so I take the car around to the front from the long-term carpark, keep reminding myself to go slow, you can drive, you know how to do this, but still this voice in my head keeps saying, *Mate, you don't have a clue, not a single idea of what might help in this situation.*

Putting Noah in the seat is unbearably hard. Too tight. Too loose. Should we call a cab? Can we take the baby back?

It's only a short drive home – our house is two blocks away, at the most – but still I take each turn super slowly, checking in the rear-view mirror to make sure he's okay.

We take the stairs. For so long, they were a necessary part of getting to our apartment, but now they seem too open, and slippery. It's cold and rainy, and I wonder if we should just move to the western suburbs where the houses sit at ground level, the entries undercover, and there's always someone near to help now you're a new dad with a brand-new baby.

# TEETHING

## New Kid

If Noah's birth was challenging, then his early days are confronting. Piece by piece, we try gainfully to reconstruct our home life; we're striving, stretching for things to be close to – if not the same as – the way they were when we entered the hospital. Only nothing is the same

There's a peanut in our room in a tiny bassinet, a bub who needs us often and for prolonged periods of time. I prepped so much to be a parent, only now, when I need to draw on any of that knowledge, it seems hopelessly generic.

I don't leave the house much except to walk him in the pram, which sits in the stairwell, two flights down from our apartment, to save us from carrying it up the stairs. Each walk I take my phone, not to stare at, but from which to play white noise in the hope that it and the motion might lull our boy to sleep. He might well be sleeping on those walks. He might also be thinking, *Why on earth does my dad keep playing noise into my cot while I'm trying to sleep?*

It's a surreal experience to be that anchored to your home (this is pre-pandemic of course), unable to go out but for an hour of physical activity, and mostly locked down in a three-bedroom apartment. I think often about the uniqueness of it – it's a world I'd been fearful of entering, for how it might irreparably shape my ability to cope with all that's required of me.

The only other times I get out are to see my dad. Annaya's

parents come over to ensure the necessary parenting coverage, and from there I head to Shenton Park rehab, watching Dad like a hawk, knowing he won't fully be making sense just yet but hoping for some slivers of him that might surface that I can mark as 'the old dad'. Even then, I know that neither he nor I are the same. Even then, I wish I could tell him how much I need him right now; say, 'I don't know how to be a dad, and was hoping you could teach me.'

Noah typically wakes early each morning, so I take him out to the living room to help his mum get some sleep. These are some of my favourite moments in early fatherhood. Watching the sun rise as I cuddle my baby. Talking to him, wondering what he's thinking, a moment so sweet, so tender, until the point that his smile switches to a grimace, a bottom-burp let loose like lava from the bubbling mouth of Krakatoa, a blue line struck with force across the front of his nappy (they call it the 'high-water mark' for a reason), and quite possibly, a brown smear up the back.

Harder for me is the ushering in of a new kind of fashion. Nappies, onesies, swaddle cloths. The cloths, in particular, can piss a person right off – some origami, do-it-yourself nonsense. I mean how exactly do you fold a swaddle cloth to keep your baby warm and wrapped? I still don't know. I don't think anyone knows or will ever know. And if I ever meet Gary Swaddle or the Swaddle family, or whoever is responsible for this cloth-based approach to bub management, I will let them know in no uncertain terms.

Onesies are better, and worse. Given babies' propensity to bust out poos like US military interventions, why do we need tight-fitting fabric that close to the deployment? There's no hiding that battle of poo, or the fabric lost along the way. Most mornings with Noah may start with a sunrise, but they end, more often than not, with a dunk of the onesie in the laundry basin, and a mad scrub at the stain.

If it isn't one end with Noah, it's the other. He has colic. *The Merriam-Webster* dictionary, if you're interested, defines colic as 'a condition in which a healthy baby is uncomfortable and cries for long periods of time', which to me reeks of someone defining something as they're going through it. On the one hand, Noah Webster, creator of *An American Dictionary of the English Language*, sits patiently, pipe in hand saying, 'Can you describe the ailment?' Whereas his wife, a swaddle cloth slung over her shoulder, shouts, 'It's when the baby cries.' Noah, perplexed, asks, 'For how long a time?' at which point his wife throws a jug at his head, and says, 'For a long time, you dipshit,' and storms off.

Colic, in our dictionary, means Noah crying incessantly. Usually, the only time he stops is when he wants to throw up, which is understandable, because it hurts and he's crying, and in the end, I think, *I might have a cry too, mate, if that's alright with you.*

It's hard knowing a baby has no power over any of this. It's daunting to think I'm supposed to get him out of things. To stop him from crying. To dry his wet tush. To tie knots –

I mean knots, of all things – to ensure he's not cold, naked or otherwise in distress.

And so, I carry on, his swaddle cloth my latest fashion accessory, with a green, blue and white striped muslin draped over my right shoulder.

Today, Noah goes for the upchuck record, first set, I've decided, by Albert 'Queasy' Jones, a blueberry of a baby that had a knack for big yacks in the 1920s. As for whether I'd rather Noah was pooing or chucking, can I say neither? Is it naïve or idealistic to say I'll take just the baby?

After three or four volcanoes, with two up top, and two moist, expressive burps down below, I take him to a café that's necessarily nice in order to offset the hot mess of my life. I sit there, half asleep, jiggling Noah in an embarrassingly loose cloth. Put him down in his pram ever so gently and head to the water station when a woman comes up and says, 'We're table number three.'

I say, 'Okay,' and smile.

She waits, motions expectingly.

'Ah,' I say, and then stare into the distance. But she stays, waiting. 'Hmm?'

'The table's dirty. I was wondering if you could give it a wipe.'

It's then I remember the cloth on my shoulder, and laugh. 'Oh, I'm not a waiter!' I say. 'It's a baby.' I point to Noah. 'Baby.'

'Your baby?'

I don't know what she thinks I'm doing out here, with a swaddle cloth on my shoulder and someone else's baby.

'Our baby.'

'How old?'

I squint, deep in thought. 'I don't know. What day is it?'

'It's Wednesday,' she says. 'October fifth. Twenty thirteen.' She says the last bit as though I'm an alien.

By this point someone's wiped her table, and it's my turn to motion to her that she's good to go.

She walks away quickly. I say, 'Thank you,' but I want to say, *Help*.

In time, I learn all kinds of things, like how onesies have button patterns that would freak out Picasso, and that some stains may fade, but will never disappear from a baby's couture or your own. That if you're a mum and you head out with a baby, people want to fawn, but also to advise. That if you're a dad and you head out with a baby, you win an Olympic medal for doing things mums do all the time.

On the opposite side of that plus, I don't see any men other than my father-in-law and the guy at the service station in the first six months of Noah's life. It's as if they evaporate. While Annaya goes to her mother's group, I also go to her mother's group a couple of times, because, well, there isn't a dad's group to go to, and how is that even possible? How, in years of societal progress, do blokes still not know how to get a bunch of blokes together in a room without beer, cars, or sport involved?

In those early months of fatherhood, I yearn for a man to talk to about this. I hope that maybe one day they will be around – even a couple of men I can hang with from time to time, and share the journey, or someone who, like me, wants to build ways for guys to connect, and places where they can just come as they are, and talk about life honestly and openly.

More than anything else, in the early days of parenting, I feel I am drowning. Annaya, too, seems to be struggling. While my sleep cycles have been disrupted, her body's no longer her own. It hurts her to breastfeed, and expressing the milk hurts her too. While we were in hospital, there was this dogged insistence on Annaya breastfeeding whatever the consequences for her. While I'm sure this wasn't intentional, there seemed all kinds of doctrines being enforced in relation to what good mums do in relation to the baby. I'm sure that's good for a baby, and yet I'm sure it's terrible for a new mother. All that pressure enforced almost immediately on the back of an already traumatic experience. *No, no, you're doing it wrong. This is how you do it. Do it like this.*

At first, I think Annaya is tired. But slowly I come to see that it is a much bigger problem. Over time, her frustration turns to fear. We get her to a doctor who gives her medication for postnatal depression. Until that kicks in, I'm on double duties. I get most of the jobs down but I'm perpetually in an elevated state. An empty milk bottle gets cleaned, immediately. Each time Annaya wakes, I tell her to keep resting, as, while I can handle all manner of domestic tasks, my whirling, self-propelling spells of productivity will fall apart if even the slightest speck of fear, frustration or self-doubt infiltrate the space, and have me admitting that right now we're only just staying afloat.

If I could use one word to describe Noah's emotional state throughout all that, I'd say he looks worried. But then, you'd look worried too if your bum kept exploding. And you'd be terrified if your parents kept looking at you and your bum as though both were uncharted territory, which is kind of what they are.

## Home Life

I don't recall much of those early days with Noah, other than tiny snatches of memory; dancing around the dinner table with him cradled in his arms, singing Weezer's 'El Scorcho', a Hail-Mary choice in the hope it would send him to sleep; concerned looks from my mother-in-law when we answer the door in our pyjamas, whatever the time of day; mornings watching Yo Gabba Gabba and evenings watching our neighbours come and go from their apartments with an enviable freedom of will and responsibility. All up, it's a dizzying cacophony of sights and sounds, a fever dream of life-experiences, and by the time Annaya has levelled out on her medication, Noah is six months old.

We live in our apartment on the second storey of a large complex and, while it's quite spacious, there's now the feeling I am mostly alone. That feeling's not alleviated by visits from the in-laws, or the gifts that arrive, and exists alongside the more comforting knowledge that our boy is smiling, pooing and throwing up in the regular way. I see my dad, of course, only now the roles are reversed – I'm guiding his expectations for rehabilitation based on my latest conversations with doctors and telling him *he's* doing great in his new life circumstances.

I feel exhausted most days, and we're both up most nights. I'm embarrassed to admit it, but on my shifts, I often watch the iPad while I hold him, sleeping, because I can't put him down on account of his reflux.

In some distant past, what feels like a lifetime ago, but was really only months back, I was a PhD student, and going particularly well – I won the Patricia Hackett Prize for my short story, 'The Knife', and won the prize for Best Creative Work at the UWA Higher Degree by Research Achievement Awards for that same story but missed out on being present to receive it because it was too close to Noah's due date to attend the ceremony. It's only months later, but my PhD is now on hold, and I'm now a present, tired and committed parent. In such a space, I wonder how anyone does anything other than being a mum or a dad, such are the demands and the responsibilities of the role.

As primary carers for our boys, we split home duties fifty-fifty. Even with that understanding in place, it often feels as though we're missing vital coverage. Indeed, it very much seems as though two parents, however dedicated they might be, are in no way equipped to handle a newborn.

I wonder what it must have been like for my mum and dad when I was born. They already had two kids at that point and had adopted a third, and then there I was, and there we all were, all needing love, affection and attention.

If I sit in that space for even a moment from an adult point of view, all kinds of questions emerge: Which kid gets priority at what point? How to manage the baby and toddler routines alongside school and kindy drop-offs? Finally, the one that haunts me most: where did *they* as a couple exist in all that chaos? Where and when did they get to just be as individuals, and the partners they once were?

I can't really imagine it at all, and it's also likely the shared wisdom on parenting then was vastly different to now. Thoughts on necessary self-care for the parents have most probably similarly expanded. With all that in mind, my parents, for the most part, were most likely seeking survival rather than balance.

As a parent in the digital age, I am initially of the belief that we'll be able to read and research our way through any issues we encounter. It does not take long, however, to see that the books are often out of date, and the advice in websites ever-changing, and the only way we'll get through anything is to work with what's in front of us. It's a liberating space but also one designed to induce anxiety in that there is no assembly of information leading to contemplation and an eventual decision. Instead, you need an instant solution to a problem which is set to the soundtrack of a child's screams.

While normal colic has that desired level of manageability, Noah's reflux is like colic on steroids. Putting him down for a sleep requires any number of questionable, bizarre approaches. We put the noise of an aircraft hangar through the iPad in the hope it will help him settle. I prance around the bed, singing 'Birdhouse in Your Soul' in the hope that it makes his eyes go droopy. When they do, I gently place him into the cot like Indiana Jones weighing up that final stone.

I put him down into the cot. I slowly, carefully, slide my hand out from underneath him, thinking *got it, got it*, and then—

*Waaaaggggggghhhh!*

I slide my hand back underneath him. Pick him up again. Sing my song a little more calmly, at least for the first couple of times. Soon enough, he closes his eyes, so I turn up the white noise. Annaya stirs almost immediately.

'Ugh!' she says, sitting up. 'What's that noise?'

'It's "aircraft hangar,"' I yell. 'I thought it might help him sleep. Only it's a bit loud!'

'Turn it off.'

'What?'

'Turn it off!'

'We can't, he'll wake up!' But man, it's loud. 'I'll try "train,"' I say, and change the app. She listens, nods, and then falls back to sleep.

I sit with Noah, start to nod off myself, and so stand up, singing softly. Within a couple of minutes, I end up kneeling beside the cot, my hand still cradled beneath his soft, peanut-shaped body. Eventually, my arm goes to sleep, as do I, only minutes before the sun rises, and it's time to do it all again.

I would love to say I know the preciousness of this time even as it's occurring. I don't. Indeed, were it not for Annaya's postnatal depression I would likely have not stopped my studies at all, save for a week or two around the birth. It's strange to think that, when planning, I so often limit experience. Indeed, in our time together as husband and wife, it's only when our plans go to shit, and we look at each other, pulses racing, that we implicitly say, 'I love you and I'm here for you.'

We muddle through it. Still, the difficulties remain, and eventually I admit to Mum that Annaya's been struggling with postnatal depression. Soon after that, my mother heads up from Albany in the Great Southern to provide some support for her son and daughter-in-law.

What to say to a mum who raised four kids, most often alone, away from her family and childhood friends? There's not much one can say other than 'thank you'. If mums have it tough now, they most likely had it much tougher in the previous generation, with so little known about postnatal depression, and so much expected of the mother to be all things to all people.

Me and Mum sit on our second-floor balcony and Noah sits in a plastic car, fixed on the spot. He's only six months old, so while it's not going anywhere, it still makes me nervous. Noah loves it. Indeed, his yelps jolt us now and then, such is their intensity.

'You were such a quiet boy,' she says, as Noah shrieks with excitement. 'Never had a peep out of you.'

'Was I happy?'

'Always,' she says, and though I'm not sure that could possibly be true, I know it's true to her.

'What was it like, raising us all?'

'It was bloody hard work,' she says, laughing. 'You stay busy as best you can. Stop for too long and it all catches up with you.'

Memories of Mum flood back into my mind. Her skating across the linoleum to mop up a spill, and hurrying through the halls with an armful of laundry. The sizzle of three frying-pans on the go; she often cooked British staples, from bubble-and-squeak to shepherd's pie, and toad-in-the-hole.

'So, pretty hard.'

'My boy, I think you're starting to get it.'

Some nights, I get Noah to bed and I'm toast. I stay up to look at pictures of him on the phone with all the pressure removed. In such moments, I find time to gather my thoughts.

My father's accident looms large throughout. When he said I'd barely know my kids before the age of five, I had not imagined he would hardly know them either.

Dad and Alice eventually come to visit, although it's clear his brain is playing catch-up. He mixes up words sometimes, and sometimes loses the thought altogether, and I sit there, smiling as if to say, *I didn't notice.*

Sometimes, in these early days, I talk to Noah. I tell him, 'I love you, and you're going be safe, I'm your dad and I love you more than anything else in this world.'

He looks back at me as if to say, 'But do you know what you're doing?' and I don't know how to answer that, not yet, when I'm still working out exactly what we're dealing with, and how quickly I can get up to speed, so my mistakes are simply blips, and not defining life events.

# Imperfect

At some point after the birth of my son and before the completion of my PhD, a storm passes through. Now that Annaya is no longer seriously depressed, and I am back immersed in my studies, it seems I have nothing left about which to worry. And yet, I am still worried about our future, and the weeks, months and years still to come.

Returning to my studies seems the most viable approach to managing both my stress levels and existential post-partum anxiety. Only, when I return to these studies, while I'm strangely comfortable in the dark, dank but quiet surrounds of The Cave, I'm less able to clearly articulate my thoughts. Most days in the office, I spend hours wrestling with where Tim Winton's version of masculinity ends and where mine begins, and how to write a compelling family love story as told from five different points of view.

I often found myself lost in obsessive thoughts before Noah's birth, and for the most part these were strangely comforting and subject specific. My master's degree was really just a run through of my current obsessions, charting the logical intersections of neoliberalism, digital distribution, Freakonomics, and Groundswell theory as it relates to the publishing industry.

While my research dated fairly quickly – and more fool me for trying to research ebooks just as they were starting to take off – the variables of thought, were for the most part, able to be reined in depending on who had written what at a particular time. While some might have found those intersections arbitrary, to me, they made perfect sense, a way of making the indefinable accessible for the layperson with neither the time nor the interest to follow a technology evolving from week to week.

Parenting is not like that. There's no point of saturation where you can say, 'Oh, if "A" represents this, then "B" represents that.' There's little to no structure, the guidance is non-existent and the classes run long into the night, each and every night. It's like being given a how-to booklet with nothing in it, or worse, it's like getting a booklet with *everything* in it, but no clue as to the right answer, or why it's right and the others are wrong.

I wonder if there is even a 'right' way to parent. I think, more often, we just do our best with what we know and hope that, looking back, our kids will see how hard we tried, or those moments when we put their needs before our own.

Imperfection as enough. Intent as healing.

I mean, imagine that, for a second. The idea that so long as we're alive, and we are willing to be flawed, humble, and authentic with our kids, we will most often get another chance to go again and make things better. When I sit in that truth, it seems to me that it permits a lifetime of growth, and acknowledgement of inherent flaws while trying to live one's best life as a human being.

It seems so simple, stated like that. In practice, though, it seems there's always a new angle to consider, and new information to take into account, over and over, to the point of exhaustion.

In The Cave, while completing my PhD, I think a great deal about parenting. How all my lessons on manhood to that point – feel less, be self-sufficient, and establish your dominance – are useless when it comes to the education, nurturing and support of a tiny boy.

I often think Noah's birth may in fact be the beginning of me discovering a workable, personal version of manhood for my unique circumstances, as opposed to simply playing along with a pre-established, often restrictive historical definition of masculinity. I wonder if Noah's birth, and the ushering in of all his feelings might similarly open me up to a richer, more awake and emotionally attuned version of Laurie.

So, even in that obsessing around what it means to be a parent, I still see some sense of hope. Not something I want to pass on just yet, more a feeling that in Noah, and in this experience in which we've found ourselves, here might be somewhere to learn more about how to be a man in this world.

## Be Here Now

My exhaustive parental reading list eventually catches up with me, and the new information I'm reading begins to contradict the books I read earlier. It also seems I'm not alone in my anxiety struggles. On parenting forums, both post-partum depression and post-partum anxiety are common discussion topics, and yet neither seem talked about enough in greater society for new mums and dads in the weeks, months and years after having a baby. The site Pregnancy, Birth and Baby suggests one or both parents may well develop generalised anxiety, panic disorder, agoraphobia, obsessive-compulsive disorder, post-traumatic stress disorder, and social phobias, after having had a child. That's a pretty impressive grab-bag of mental health challenges for a stage that's supposedly filled with joy, awe and wonder.

My psych explains these various conditions and suggests an umbrella term – generalised anxiety – that is more appropriate for me given the current stage of my life. It's not easy to have a baby, he says. It's not easy to have a father who fell off a roof and into a coma, either. It is tough, he suggests, to complete a PhD while you're raising your first child. And it must be difficult, he says, to raise that child with your father incapacitated and your mother living miles away.

I'm already on medication – I started it before Noah was born, a bit like fastening your seatbelt after you've sat down in a biplane because you know the ride is about to get rocky – and so instead my psychologist and I work on mindfulness. He gives me a single sultana and says it's today's exercise in being present.

'Now close your eyes. What do you want to do with it?'

'I want to throw it in the bin,' I say.

'Or maybe eat it,' he suggests.

'Okay.'

'Is it wrinkly?'

'Yes.'

'Is it tender?'

What a question. It's not a Coldplay song, or a soldier who's returned from war and is about to surprise his wife with a bunch of flowers. It's just a grape gone wrinkly.

'Sure.'

'Do you feel calm?'

'No.'

'Well, focus,' he says. 'Get to know the sultana.'

I sit with the sultana for a while, though I'm not really sure it wants to be there. It's quiet, and to be honest, it's being a bit of a dick in that it doesn't ask me how I am, or ask me about the baby or anything else.

That night, as we sit in bed, prior to turning off the light I tell Annaya I'm struggling. I talk around the subject of being a dad, then say, 'It's so hard.'

She says, 'It's going to be hard.'

'You never worry?'

'I always worry.'

'What do you worry about?'

'I worry whether the meconium consumption did permanent damage to our boy's brain. I worry about my dad dying. I worry about your dad dying. I hope Noah will find friends at school. I worry that he won't. I hope you'll handle this time okay, as I know you've had anxiety in the past. I worry you'll do something stupid. I worry you'll die from a heart attack. I worry that the only thing that could tear us apart is what we're going through right now.'

'Wow.'

'Wow,' she says, and goes back to reading her book.

*I worry about that too*, I think to myself, but don't tell her. For some reason, it feels scary to be that honest, and admit we're both sitting in that same spiralling space.

I can't sleep that night. I write a piece about how I can't sleep, then do push-ups on, and right jabs against the wall, but then my knuckles start to hurt, and I think this must be the dumbest thing I've done since I bought that *Shoot Pass Slam* CD single by Shaquille O'Neal.

Having remembered my worst CD purchase, I remember one of my best, and I'm briefly soothed by the rawness and realness of Rico, a Glaswegian industrial rock singer who got me through a particularly rough patch in 1999 with his debut album, *Sanctuary Medicines*. While there are no tracks that explicitly deal with parenting, there's a bunch of angst, and a sonic soundscape comfortingly familiar to the younger me that more often felt lost rather than found. Revisiting it now is like boyhood Laurie meeting Laurie the dad in a clearing. It's hard to reconcile how much has happened since when I first heard this album as a young single man walking the streets of Aberdeen. The sparse beats of 'Float' are the singer's quiet declaration of much-needed solitude, which now seems out of reach for a dad and his bub, both so hopelessly dependent on each other.

I stay stuck in the monochrome. I make a ball of Blu-Tack. Think, does that make me crazy? I write a piece about making the ball of Blu-Tack and its links to my being crazy, that surprisingly never gets published.

I worry a lot, generally speaking. I think about calling Dad but it's too late, and anyway, he has enough problems right now, and could probably do without his adult son seeking guidance on the most self-explanatory job on the planet.

I go into my son's room, watch him sleep for a bit. He's perfect, still serene, bigger now than that tiny dot in the hospital but similarly still.

Thoughts come quietly but quickly. They're thoughts that, for the most part, have felt too scary to vocalise before this point.

*I'm worried I can't be the dad you want to be. I'm worried I'll mess this up, and I don't want to mess this up. I'm worried I will die before I get to see you be a dad. I'm worried you'll be lonely, like I was lonely.*

*I'm worried I don't know anything about any of this. I'm worried you'll get sick. I'm worried you'll get hurt. I'm worried you'll love someone who will hurt you, and from there, you'll lose faith in the power of love.*

*I'm worried about whether I'll find a job after my PhD. I'm scared something will happen to you out there. I'm scared something will happen to you in here; that we'll say the wrong thing or make the wrong decision, and it will change your life in ways we could never have imagined.*

*I thought I could get around all of these things if I could stay untethered, me and no one else. But I'll try. I'll do everything I can to find the hope, hold it close every day.*

As I stand by his bed and worry, he lies quietly sleeping. I watch his chest rise, up and down, and my anxiety subsides, at least to the point that I can go to sleep tonight and work the rest out tomorrow.

# Fleeting

After those intense early months, Annaya and I fall mostly into a pattern of cuddles, cots and reflection.

Some days, Noah still won't sleep on account of the reflux, and our flat's too small, and I feel lost and alone. Many days I find us driving with Noah, driving past Kinross, Clarkson and Butler – suburbs that didn't even exist when I was young – as a way to get him to sleep.

We're not yet out of the suburban sprawl, despite having driven north for twenty minutes straight. We stop at monolithic shopping malls with the good sense not to be open so late on a Sunday. We head into petrol stations, we buy bottles of water and packets of chips, to make up for the meal we'll miss while we're driving around to get Noah to sleep.

I keep my humour for the most part, determined not to give in to despair. Annaya continues to breastfeed, continually in pain from the bitey-ness of it all. She says, 'Remember Barcelona?' as we reach the end of the freeway. I say, 'It's great, but it's no Alkimos,' and we laugh, although we want to cry.

While Annaya's no longer suffering from postnatal depression, she's still exhausted, and worried, and sore from all the biting, and it often feels as though we are no longer a part of our city or state. We're either at home, at the nearest cafe, or at a vaccination appointment for Noah, all of which are within a block of our apartment complex. On Annaya's birthday, we walk to a fancier café that's two blocks away instead of one. For late brunch, we feed Noah fingers of toast, and only make it through half our coffees before again he gets restless, and it's time to go home.

Months later, coming into spring, and sometimes when we've finally got Noah down, we head to the balcony, pushing aside the foldable clothes airer so we can sit and not be covered in damp swaddle-cloths. The airer rolls momentarily, hits the air-con unit and squeaks with contentment.

We sit, and in the world outside our apartment, lights twinkle on the other side of Lake Joondalup. Get closer, and I'd imagine they'd be streets of cookie-cutter houses, but from here, they look like earthbound stars.

A couple of years ago, a man got stuck in that lake. He'd attended a concert nearby and while walking home had tried to cut across it, as it often goes dry over Perth's hot summers. Only it wasn't dry enough that summer, it was sludge, and well, he'd misjudged the whole thing, and was knee-deep in muck, with no means of escape.

This comes back to me as I sit on the only place in our home where I can rest without the fear of having to immediately get up again.

My brother Trent visits for a coffee a couple of weeks later, having completed a stay in rehab. I saw him a couple of times while he was there, and he seemed better there than he does when out with the general public. It's something both my father and I have noticed: all three of us could walk into the same pub; only Trent would have somehow spotted the dodgy bloke in there and started up a conversation or an alliance.

Dad suggests I not share one of my more recently published short stories, 'The Knife', with Trent – it taps into a shared history of losing friends while we were young – in case it triggers him back to using. Instead, I bring my baby boy, grateful for a chance for my older brother to see the nephew he missed while he was getting clean.

'How you doing?'

'You know,' he says. 'Like what am I even going to do now? I guess I just do it, right?' He nods, as if attempting to anchor the thought, and that hope. 'But man, look at you. You got it together, bro.'

'That could be you too, mate. The world is yours if you want it, you know?'

He waves me away as if I've suggested he could fly to the moon if only he could put his mind to it. 'Maybe one day. You think a thug could find a girl?'

'*Thug*. Bro, not even Tupac was a thug. You know that, right? You heard what happened on the set of *Poetic Justice*?'

'Things blow up? He had to smack someone?'

'Well things blew up, but that's not the important part. Maya Angelou, she's this poet, right? She writes some beautiful stuff. Man, you should read it some day. Anyway, she's on the set, and Tupac's there on the first day, cussing like nobody's business. Then, day two, a fight breaks out, and an older guy takes one of the men away, and Maya, she takes Tupac with her, walks him down away from the crowd. He's arguing with her, all combative, and she says, "No, let me talk to you, please."

'Eventually, she calms him down, and says, "Do you know how much you're needed? Do you know how important you are to us?"'

'Stop it, Lor, you'll make me cry.'

'Well, that's what Tupac does. He cries, and she faces him away from the people on the set so he won't get embarrassed, and then she dries the tears on his cheek with her hand.'

'Man,' says Trent.

'I know, right? That's everyone. How important you are, how much you matter to the world if you can just be real, and show up, and give love, as best you can. Hey, you want to hold Noah?'

'Nah, mate, you're okay.'

'Come on, hold him,' I say, and hand him over. He looks nervous for a bit, but then holds him up, in front of his chest, as if presenting a trophy.

I can't imagine how it feels to hold a baby when you know you weren't held by your own mum for too long before ending up in hospital. I know it's doing something to him in this moment, though. Knowing he was once a baby and had to make it on his own from so early on. All these nurses doing their best to lessen the impact of being in a ward, instead of at home, for nearly the first three years of his life.

When we get back to our apartment, I give Noah to Annaya and pour us glasses of cold water from the fridge.

'You're scared, hey?'

'Mm,' says Trent.

I lead him over to the bookshelf. There's a dusty selfie of me and him. We took it in 2007, three months before I met Annaya. I'd come back from the east coast of Australia after a particularly painful break-up. At some point, I had to drive from York, where I was staying with Dad, to Perth to take my stuff out of storage, and back home to Dad's. To do this, I needed to drive to Perth in a car to pick up the hire truck, drive to Forrestfield to unload the storage container, drive back to York to drop off my belongings, drive back to Perth to drop the truck, and drive the car back to York one last time.

No one in the world had volunteered to help out with that particular task except for Trent, who said 'Sure' without hesitation when I asked him. We drove back and forth for around eight hours that day and took a sweaty pic on my phone at arm's length when we were done. The craziest thing about the photo is that we're stoked at the end of such a crazy, tiring day, and bound as brothers on account of having shown up so profoundly for each other.

'Here we go,' says Trent. 'What's the lesson?'

'This picture,' I say, ignoring him, 'is from six years ago. I was heartbroken, man, like bottom of the barrel, you know? Still, at some point I had to face facts; we'd broken up for good, and I had to get my stuff out of storage. I asked around. Dad's got a bad back, I can't get Luke on the phone, and my mates? Man, I've never heard so many excuses.

'But not you. You were just there. That's what brothers do,

right? And that guy, the guy who showed up that day, *that* is the real Trent. That's who you can be every day. It takes work, but that guy, he's the best. He's my big brother. I love him, and I love you.'

'I love you too, baby bruvs,' he says, one final hug and back slap. He's heading down south, staying with my mum and sister, and this time, hoping to stay clean for good.

That evening, I'm a little emotional, as I often am after time with Trent. I sit next to Annaya and Noah on the couch. He's in the corner, propped against a cushion, wearing an aqua-striped shirt and a Winnie the Pooh disposable nappy.

'You think he's going to make it?'

'I don't know,' says Annaya. 'But he's an adult now, yeah? At some point, life becomes less about what happened to you, and more about what you do on the back of it.'

'I know. Still, it's hard.'

Noah giggles.

'What do you think? He loved seeing you.'

Noah says. 'Gug,' and puts three fingers in his mouth, I tickle him and the giggles get louder.

'Such a cutie,' says Annaya to me, a declaration, as though we've not previously noted how fricking adorable our baby boy is, or the way in which he balances out the tough times, the sadness and grief whenever my mind wanders, or I'm caught thinking too much about endings rather than beginnings.

# Brothers

I decided early on in my life that I would not have children. I figured, being the youngest of three boys, that no one would notice either way.

My decision had not been made out of fear, or, at least, it seemed that way at the time. I don't know why I had been so concrete in my thoughts, either. For whatever reason, parenthood simply did not seem part of my future. In my mind, I was more like Uncle Travelling Matt, sending postcards to his nephew Gobo in the TV show *Fraggle Rock*.

Upon reflection, it may not have been Matt's childlessness that called to me, but rather his curiosity about the outside world. Indeed, when I watch these episodes now, there's something of a paternal relationship between Matt and Gobo. In the episode, 'Sidewalk Creatures', Matt's postcard talks about getting to know creatures that are actually parking machines, though he's not aware of that. He writes how he fed one of the creatures and may now have a new friend. He hopes so, anyway, as he admits he gets lonely travelling the world. The scene then cuts back to Gobo reading the postcard out loud, and when it gets to that final line about feeling lonely, Gobo's visibly affected, and acknowledges that he gets lonely too.

As a son and now a father, I so often loop back to that reality of loneliness. Perhaps my identification with Uncle Matt then and now is as much about someone admitting they get lonely instead of forever pretending things are fine, just as they are.

My experience of older brothers, given they were three and five years older than me, again fed into these feelings of loneliness. To be clear, Trent and Luke were great brothers, it's just I felt (and indeed was) both younger and quite different from them.

My eldest brother, Luke, was a natural-born leader: funny, charismatic, and happy to take us into the fray of a doomed trip up a hill through countless pockets of brambles on the way there, and steep, difficult climbs over cliff faces on the way back, on one of which we nearly lost Trent. As a boy, he handmade his own crime chapbooks, the Victor Drago series, with us on the front covers as thugs, and bullets, guns and knives drawn on the back alongside a list of other titles in the series. It's possible, and indeed likely, that these stories began my own interest in the power of storytelling.

Trent also played a pivotal, mostly unsung part in my development as a writer, and from my fifth birthday onwards, he regaled me with stories each night about a superhero called Granny, and Rangi, a proud Māori teenager and protector of the people. We also breakdanced together as a two-man posse, and if you managed to track down footage of our one public concert, you'd see that Trent blew the roof off with his donkey kicks, windmills and hurricanes.

Trent struggled in his teenage years and by his twenties he was more a ghost, albeit one with occasional moments of lucidity or welcome good humour. Mostly, though, I lost the Trent I'd loved as a kid and welcomed a more detached, dissociated brother. There were no more stories to tell or memories to revisit, it seemed, and in the time we spent together I was mostly his keeper, his taxi or his apologist.

My eldest brother, Luke, also struggled, but got help at a pivotal point. Like me, he set up support structures to ensure his setbacks don't turn into catastrophes. Which is not to say that Luke's struggles don't greatly affect him, or me. While we'd both like to think we could reach out in a crisis, we rarely do because our struggles make it harder to connect, or reach back, without a spike in anxiety, or the fear we'll be judged or misunderstood.

We're luckier than Trent in so many ways, and it's not as though there aren't any number of contributing factors to his downhill trajectory. The stability of those first formative years is vital for any child. And, while I sometimes wonder how my life would have been without Trent – at the very least, I would have had a room of my own, and more attention in the family home – I also know my struggles are fundamentally different to that of a child who has been adopted.

While Luke and I are not thick as thieves, I have a great deal of affection and respect for my eldest brother. Luke's a deep thinker, and we enjoy sharing theories, research and philosophy. Growing older, we've found a shared love of independent and arthouse cinema (though differing in tone and genre), and we're humanists to the core, often settling on the importance of care and compassion over greed or self-interest.

We're also both creative: I write books, he writes music, and we talk a lot about art and creativity. Now that we both have kids, we revel in the opportunities to be there for our boys. His sons are now roughly the same age as he and I were when our parents split up.

As parents, we're pretty much on the same page. While we're aware of the need to set boundaries and educate our kids on the dangers out in the world, we also see fatherhood as a fun, healing space. No longer do we need to play video games on our own when there's a kid who can't wait to play with us. Car rides are now opportunities to introduce our boys to our favourite bands from years past, and cuddles are on tap for our sons should they need them. In short, we hope our presence is a giant bandaid, and a chance, when needed, to let our kids know they're *the* most important thing in the room and in our lives.

Luke played guitar like a god in his teens, and with his long hair, shredded jeans and sleeveless tees, he was cool in a Metallica kind of way. In my childhood, his favourite bands echoed through our house: Alice Cooper, Motörhead and even 'Killer Queen' one night, although he'd likely be loath to admit it. I only remember hearing the song on that particular night because I thought, *Wow, this is heaps better than 'Killed by Death'.*

Soon after that Luke was out of the family home, having moved in with a girl, and her newborn baby nearby. I saw him from time to time in the years that followed, and it seemed that he, like me, was determined to make things work with each girlfriend he found.

These weren't the idle dalliances of lovestruck teenagers.

For me and him, these moments were a chance to fix what was broken; an opportunity to change the script, and find enduring, healing love.

When Luke had his own son, Eli, almost fifteen years after leaving home, my immediate thought was how natural a dad he was, and so steady with a bub in his arms.

In my favourite picture from that time, I'm cradling Eli in my arms. I'm not smiling. I'm awestruck by the little dude and the way in which he stares back at me. On that day, maybe the seeds of my resistance were sown. Maybe it was then when I considered I might one day feel stable and centred enough to bring a child into the world.

I wouldn't have a son for another ten years. I loved seeing Luke blossom in his new role, though. While their story is not mine to tell, Luke and Ayla's bub was something of a miracle, and when he showed up, you couldn't help but be touched by his presence, or the way in which Luke changed in the face of having become a dad.

In watching Luke, I had a preview of parenthood. Watching him, I saw it wasn't as bad as I had feared it would be. I'd figured parenting would be hard, whatever the composition of kids or parents on board. Looking at Luke, no longer so defined by his past, I wondered whether I might have access to that same possibility. I found myself open not just to becoming a dad, but to ongoing commitment with a family of my own, remaining open to the future, however it presented itself. I worried about how my anxiety might coexist with the new challenges of parenting but, when my turn actually came, I felt fatherhood changing me. If nothing else, my more anxious tendencies were kept at bay because I needed to survive for someone other than myself, and to nurture them through their most vulnerable time.

We're nine months into parenting when Luke and Eli come to see us at our Joondalup apartment. That delay is understandable; Luke's not great at getting out at the best of times. I'm also typically the one who organises our catch-ups, so with all that's been going on, it took that long to just come up for air, let alone be awake enough and forward-thinking enough to proactively encourage visitors.

Noah perks up immediately in their presence. Luke's voice goes up an octave, it's softer than usual. Noah flashes his trademark smile, Luke laughs, and it strikes me that I love to hear my brother laugh.

'I can't believe you're a dad, bro!'

'Arrgh,' I say, laughing. 'I don't know what I'm doing.'

'Nobody does,' says Luke. 'Just do your best, and keep on going, and then one day they've shot right up, isn't that right, Eli?'

Eli looks confused. 'Huh?'

'You rascal!' says Luke, in mock exasperation, and pulls him in for a hug, so that Eli's head is in Luke's armpit.

I stare across at my brother, grinning, and his kind, genuine son, wedged in a playful headlock. They seem so happy, and so rested, and I think, *Maybe I'll get through this after all.*

# DEPARTURE

# A Simple Truth

In 2014, I am selected for my first competitive writers' residency since the birth of Noah, and a chance to revisit my PhD away from the pressures of parenting. In attending, I'll also be the first Australian Fellow in the history of the Elizabeth Kostova Foundation's Sozopol Fiction Seminars. I'll be there for just over two weeks, first in Sofia, the capital city of Bulgaria, and then in Sozopol, a seaside town on the southern Bulgarian Black Sea coast. Having postponed my PhD studies for six months when Noah was born, this feels like the perfect opportunity to reconnect with my writing.

I approach this residency with some trepidation. I am afraid my old life as a writer, the one I so carefully curated, has already been replaced by the new and relentless role of fatherhood.

More than that, I know how big a deal it is to have been selected for Sozopol in the first place. Alongside five Bulgarian writers, they pick five other writers from around the world. So, of course, I'm excited about it, and yet at the same time I feel ill-equipped for this opportunity. So, in the lead-up to the seminars, I'm metaphorically splashing cold water on my face, over and over, saying, 'Come on, man, you can do this!'

The night before I leave, I'm already exhausted. I'm sick even before I fly out but keep working on my PhD right until the day of the flight. From there, things go according to plan, at least until I'm in Bulgaria. The first flight (from Perth to Singapore) is completed in short order. The second, from Singapore to Germany, departs three hours later, is much longer and by the time I get to Frankfurt, I feel grotty and worn out.

When we finally touch down, I take a cab from the airport to the middle of Sofia. At the hotel, I decide that this is the time, my time to get my career back on track, and it's then that a familiar voice returns and says, *Okay, we do this, now. I'm counting on you.*

I call this voice the inner critic and it's been with me for much of my life. It's here to help me, or at least, that's what I tell myself. Or maybe that's the story it tells me. Sometimes, it's hard to tell the difference.

My inner critic manifested as responsibility through high school, where I ended up being a student councillor and eventually a prefect, and through any number of menial jobs I worked while studying my first two degrees. It resurfaced when I broke up with the girl I dated before Annaya, in early 2007. When I could barely get out of bed, it said, *Come on, get up. It's time to work out what we're going to do next. That's the deal, remember?*

When I decided to apply for my master's degree in publishing and editing, it said, *That's good, we'll go there and meet people who can make your dreams a reality.* Then, as I worked nights on my master's research project, it said, *This is worth the sacrifice. Maybe send a couple of emails, though; see if you can talk to some industry professionals.*

While I had quelled my inner critic to some degree on the back of getting into a scholarship program at UWA, there still seemed an understanding that I would continue to push myself in all things writing as and when needed. And, in the case of the Sozopol Seminars it meant applying year after year until I was selected.

My inner critic only has my back, it seems, until the point where things go wrong. At that stage, it does one of two things: it raises the bar, insisting I go again and again until reaching my next achievement. Or it's a ghost, and I feel alone and abandoned.

In Bulgaria, and for the first time in my life, my inner critic no longer seems so vital to my drive or my continued sense of self-confidence. If anything, it feels intrusive, and its perpetual criticism feels like a block to enjoying this moment. Despite that, I think, *You've got this, Laurie. I mean Christ, you're one of only five English-speaking writers selected in the world. How cool is that?*

Evidently, not cool enough.

*So, what's next?* it says. *How do we make the best of this opportunity?*

What do you mean? I made it here, right?

*I know, but you're surrounded by editors and industry professionals from around the world. You write short stories. So, here's the deal: you get a story placed, we'll call it a success.*

I just want to meet people.

*I'm sorry, what?*

I want to meet them, and get to know them, and—

*That's not a thing. Also, you don't fly halfway across the world just to meet people. You do it to change your life. Remember Iowa?*

Yes.

*And you worked on 'The Knife', and it changed your life, didn't it?*

Yes.

*So, now you have a kid, and you know you can't do any of this once you're back home. So do it now. They chose you, Laurie. Are you the mistake in their selection process?*

No. I never said—

*The clock is ticking. Get some painkillers, some nasal spray, and we'll sort the rest out later.*

For the first week in Sofia, and the next week and a half at the fiction seminars on the coast at Sozopol, I forge connections with the other four English-speaking Fellows. They're all super-nice, all doing more prestigious programs than me, and none have children. I connect more organically with the Bulgarian Fellows as many of them have kids, or are studying and working at the same time, or they write when they can, mostly only once the kids have gone to bed.

I wear a business shirt, dress shoes and trousers every day in an effort to look my most professional. I clash with one of the English-speaking Fellows, a writer called Kali, who wears a green vinyl jacket, hosts her own regular spoken word event, and has been published in *McSweeney's*, *The Paris Review* and *Electric Literature*.

I try to meet her in a professional sense. I tell her I enjoyed reading about her spoken word events, and that it's great to see less pretentious events coming up. She gets offended, says, 'Oh, mine is pretentious. It's necessarily pretentious,' and it's clear I've misjudged, well, everything.

I want to crawl into a hole. Everything I'd like to say, from 'Good on you! I wish I had the gumption to wear a vinyl jacket, and pull it off,' to 'I read one of your stories, Kali, and it was incredible, I loved it,' seem pointless now she's seen through my plans of appearing cold and analytical as the hapless, hopeless meanderings of a social dunce.

My inner critic loves that feeling of dissonance. *You wanted to meet your competition*, it says. *Well, that's your competition. Right now, I'd say she has you beat.*

For the rest of the seminars, it's not even about Kali, it's just me and my inner critic, with me doing all I can to seize opportunities. I meet the editor of one of the United States' best literary journals over breakfast and, later that day, we are given the opportunity to book a consultation session to discuss our stories or chapters. I book him in for later that evening and then wonder what to submit.

*Something polished. Something complete*, says my inner critic.

In the end, I go for my story, 'Twenty-eight Steps', a how-to-grieve guide from one brother to another, as presented in dot points. I send it straight away. We've arranged to talk after dinner, at around eight thirty, so that will give him plenty of time to read my work and formulate his thoughts and feedback.

Instead, halfway through the meal, he comes over to my booth, waiting. Once he has my attention, he motions to the hallway, and so we walk there quickly, me with my notebook and him with a printout of my story.

'Laurie—' He pauses. 'I don't know what this is.'

'What do you mean?'

'This,' he says, holding the paper up in front of him, before letting his arm fall to his side. 'It's not a story.'

'Oh.'

'Man, I want to help you, but you need to send me *something*,' he says. 'Not now, though. This, it's done. But next time, send me a story, okay?'

'Okay,' I say, and then he's gone.

Soon after that, I meet the advisor of another well-regarded literary journal over dinner. I get on better with her than the previous editor, and she asks me to submit to her journal for publication, only this time there's no consultation or feedback process. She says to email her directly and from there, she'll get the ball rolling.

I send it to her. She emails me back. She says the story is not right for the journal. I pore back over the words, but can't I see what's wrong, or how to fix it.

I meet one final editor who's in charge of a high-profile industry publication. He loves the idea for my novel *You Belong Here*. He's enthusiastic and he wants to read the novel when it's ready. While he can't read my stories for consideration as he's not in that kind of role, he's happy he met me, and for a moment I think that might be enough. Later that day, the seminar coordinator, Maryam, comes to find me having emailed the Fellows days earlier about introducing Bulgaria's esteemed writer and literary icon, Dragan Nikolov, when he speaks to the group. As of yet, no one has put up their hand. She thinks I would be perfect and would be delighted if I accept the opportunity.

The next day I see Kali talking with the two people who rejected my work, and the one who seemed to like it. I call Noah and Annaya on Skype soon after that. Annaya asks how I'm going, and I lie, and say I'm doing great, and all the while my boy keeps touching the screen.

This time – and for the first time in my life – it is hard to be away from home. I'm anxious not only for my career but also at the thought of being so far away from the ones I love. Worrying that something might happen, and I wouldn't be there to protect them. Watching my love and my baby boy on a screen, wishing I could just step through it and be back with them. Wanting to tell them they're my world, and my Achilles heel some days, as I strive to be a father and a writer.

Only of course, I don't tell them that. I just say, 'I'd better go.'

When I get to the hotel cafe, Dragan Nikolov sits there, big and bearded, like a grumpy Santa Claus. When he sees me, though, he gets up, holds my hand with both of his, and smiles, speaking quickly in Bulgarian.

'You came to meet me. You will introduce me,' says the translator.

'It is an honour. Such a great writer,' I reply, and again the translator kicks in.

The back and forth, awkward at first, until soon enough, it slips into sharing; thoughts, feelings, hopes and dreams. For the next hour, I'm closer to being present than at any other time on the trip. We sit, hands clasped, a young man and elder statesmen, with neither speaking the other's language, and the translator doing double time.

I tell him I have a child, and I fear I will mess it all up.

He tells me for so long it was hard to hope for his country, and for the future.

I say I must write to survive, and sometimes I'm not sure if Annaya knows that.

He says we must always write with our souls, and never be afraid to be real on the page.

At some point we both start to cry, and then we laugh, communicating through the translator, our slightly different versions, first of 'Look at me, so silly to be crying,' and then laughing without need for translation.

He meets my gaze one final time, and says, by translation, 'Thank you for coming. Some people are afraid to meet me. They think I am a lion. Maybe I act big, only maybe I am caring, also, and still want to connect. To speak and be heard.'

'I hear you,' I say.

'So, be you!' he says theatrically, and releases my hands, laughing.

*But which me?* I want to ask. *Which one gets me where I so desperately need to go?*

By the final night of the trip, my inner critic has stopped talking to me other than to say, *This will not do*, and to tell me, yet again, that I must figure out a way to get back on track.

On the night of the final dinner, in Sofia, I'm done with dressing up. Dragan's deep voice still lingers in my thoughts, his eyes twinkling back at me; all that curiosity and compassion within one man; forever finding purpose in passion, perfection in how words illuminate ideas and echo out into a greater philosophy and way of looking at the world.

I put away my blazer, my trousers, and my button-up shirt and instead slip on some jeans and a hoodie. I get to the restaurant late, and when I arrive, everybody's in a huddle, talking, including Kali in her green vinyl jacket.

I tap her on the shoulder. She turns around, smiles a smile I haven't seen this trip.

'It's you,' she says, and this time I know what that means.

*It's you, and you're no longer so hung up on fulfilling your duties.*

*It's you, now that we're out of time, and there's no way I can really get to know you.*

*It's you, and you messed things up, and yet you know on some level I could give a shit where you've been published; you just seemed like a good guy, like someone I could talk to.*

Back at the hotel, I pack for tomorrow's flight, and keep hearing Kali's voice. She's saying, 'Why this story? Why now? And why should I care?'

Why *should* she care? I don't know. She just did, and maybe still does, and it's this simple truth I hold onto as I fly home: all the moments I missed to be me while I was trying to be perfect.

# Passing Time

The Graduate Research School passes both the creative and critical components of my PhD at The University of Western Australia in July 2015. In many ways, I'm sad to say farewell to my PhD studies. While I know other tasks demand my time – not least the ongoing care of Noah, nearly two years old by this point – contact with my supervisors both before and after Noah's birth always felt particularly grounding. The tertiary landscape has also fundamentally shifted since I started my PhD only four years earlier. At that time, I had hoped to become a lecturer at UWA upon completing my PhD. By the time I've completed my studies, two of my alumni Arts faculties have shrunk to less than half their size , and there's increasing reliance on sessional academics to take up the teaching slack with only a week or two's notice prior to the start of semester. Although permanent teaching roles at a tertiary level are still occasionally advertised, I'm told quite clearly, by those who would know, to steer clear of them on account of the increased pressures and responsibilities for the modern Australian full-time academic.

I spend most days with Noah, and others in consultation about an upcoming ankle reconstruction. The ligaments that should have been holding my ankle in place perished three decades ago, after I played a game of footy on a twisted ankle injured early in the first quarter. It had swollen up so much by the end of the game that they had to cut my boot off with scissors. In the years after, my foot would occasionally give way completely as I walked along the street. Team sports had long been abandoned for the need to survive, and so part-time jobs at fast-food chains and cafes took priority over exercise.

I meet with a doctor who's very good but too expensive. We try another; he's cheaper but seems distracted, and I hope he's good enough not to hit a nerve, or otherwise cause further damage. By the end of an appointment, we're booked in for surgery; my foot will finally be brought back to its original strength, or something like it, more than twenty years after it was first injured.

Before the surgery happens, I drive an hour and a half east to the golden fields of my father's home in York.

It's hard to get a half-decent coffee in York, except at Cafe Bugatti. There was once a DVD shop but that closed down, and in terms of global dining, there is a Chinese restaurant. Vegetarians, like me, can go to Jules Shoppe, which is far from the land of roasts, spuds and gravy, and whose falafels are so crunchy and yet tender that they could just about make you move to the wheatbelt then and there.

It feels as though my dad has lived here forever. York is a bit like that. You go when you find time, and yet it also feels like a place where time has stopped. The motor museum, which I first visited when I was nine years old, is still there, as are the main pubs, the Castle, the Imperial and Settlers House, although the Imperial can't seem to find a reliable owner and so switches from open to closed to open on a regular basis. Through it all, my dad lives here, and was a general practitioner at large until his accident. The times since have been interesting – he's found a love of rocks he never had, a sincerity that was rarer in my younger years and he's dropped a ton of weight.

Cognitively, he's doing better, but occasionally slips. There's the odd word he can't annunciate, or a phrase whose meaning he misinterprets. We're told that's to be expected for someone who has undergone major brain trauma.

Dad and I talk about all kinds of things from philosophy to politics. More often than not, our main topic is happiness, and there are reams and reams of printed email correspondence from my twenty-third to twenty-eighth birthdays on that subject.

He favours kindness, gratitude and compassion. I ask, B*ut what if you've been hurt, and you no longer know if you can trust that being kind makes a difference?*

*It makes a difference, always*, he writes. And then he finishes, with Love, Dad, the same way every time, with 'Love' coming first, and 'Dad' on the next line.

Many a morning, we go to Bugatti's, run by Lisa, who keeps counter up front, and Tony, the chef, out back. Because it's a Saturday when I visit, Dad and I head over to the big table near the front window – it's the round one with all the blokes around it.

This is the Breakfast Club, an irrepressible band of seniors from York and surrounds. I already know town journalist

Giles – out of nowhere, he took a photo of me sitting at this very cafe when I came home from Melbourne having completed my master's degree. The headline, 'Local Boy Makes Good', made me laugh, as I'm at best an interloper and infrequent guest at this table of men.

It's never the exact same configuration at any of these breakfasts, and so I meet a dazzling array of folks: chemists, farmers and real estate professionals. Blokes near retirement, and those keen to talk nest eggs and superannuation.

'G'day, young fella,' is their typical greeting. I'm a mate by association, as any son of the great Dr Steed automatically gets a free pass.

Almost all of them shake my hand as if they're trying to pull a branch from a tree. There are many laughs, all of them genuine, and I wonder if this is the loss that lies at the heart of my generation of men: face-to-face interaction in a safe, real space among friends.

They talk of crops, weather, and real estate, often also dipping into federal politics or local council matters. They are unequivocally engaged in their world; in my space of irony, cleverness and cool detachment I feel conversationally bereft. I'm not sure I've ever known how to care that much about the world, as opposed to a book, an album or a kick-arse video game.

The other thing that stays with me is their unique type of knowledge. When talking of practical things their knowledge is absolute and learned through years of lived experience. Your alternator is skipping? They know what to do. Your table needs stripping back and revarnishing? They'll tell you the grade of sandpaper required. And, if you've got yourself bogged, don't even sweat it, they'll be there with a ute and a towrope before you can say, 'It's okay, fellas, there's nothing to see here.'

On Saturdays, most of the Breakfast Club head on to the Men's Shed. I go there while in town as if I'm lancing a boil, and almost break into hives from the sheer practicality of the place. These are machines, oils and lubricants I've seen only briefly in films like *Over the Top* and *Flashdance*. I don't think they dance here, however. I watch for a while as Dad mingles, moving from station to station. He picks up things they've made from wood and metal.

I wonder, for a second, if you could make these with a 3D printer.

Later, over a cup of tea, an older man with silver stubble and cavernous cheeks tells me how his son and daughter-in-law bunged up their toilet. He talks me through its dismantling, what was stuck and how he got it unstuck. He goes into exquisite detail, so much so that I wonder if I can ask him about parenting. Whether it might also be as simple as that. A tweak here and an adjustment there, and you're back in business.

I leave my father to it as it's clear he's in his element, as listener, nurturer and confidante. I'm not sure what they make of me, a man with four degrees but no idea of how to sand back a table or fix a bracket to a wall. So much of the knowledge I gleaned in those first three degrees – from film studies to journalism to editing and publishing – shifted on the back of the digital revolution. So many jobs for which I was undoubtedly trained at the time needed new requirements and software proficiencies by the time I had graduated.

At both the Breakfast Club and the Men's Shed, it's not lost on me I'm allowed entry based solely on my gender. That is one thing I think our generation does much better than theirs, as it's not for me, that level of overt exclusion. Still, I'd rather these older men were here, debating current affairs and building furniture, and not pissing their feelings up against a wall in a pub or sitting alone, slowly growing older and lonelier.

For them, it works. With so many other roles and responsibilities in their life, they need a place where being a 'bloke' is a strength. It's not how I would do things. But then, they made it for them, not me– a generation of men whose experience of manhood is quite different to my own.

Driving back to the tin roof and many dogs of Dad's place – Alice nurses refuge greyhounds back to full health – thoughts come of whether I'm blessed or cursed to have been raised by my mother and sister, rather than my practical dad.

Seeing those men in their shed, I felt strangely alien. And yet, inside of me a longing remained, not for these men and their machines, but for a supportive community of my own. A place where I could go and be myself. Where flaws are welcomed, and indeed, where they form the beginning of our most vital conversations.

My aim for this trip was partly to talk to Dad about Jeremy, as I've been undertaking a therapy called Eye Movement

Desensitisation and Reprocessing, focusing specifically on the memory of Jeremy's death. At first, I find that recollecting the events of that time is frightening, because Jeremy's death was difficult enough the first time around. Still, that's all I've been doing for years: going over and over things since the day I found out that he'd died. I have thought a lot about the impact his loss had on me at such a young age, and the ball of grief that I still carry and so, eventually I surrendered to the suggestion of my psychologist to let him help me with my pain.

I tell Dad about my recent experiences with EMDR. The idea, I say, is for the memories to no longer come up as frequently, or as intensely.

'Crazies, the lot of them,' he says.

'Hmm?'

'Psychiatrists,' he says.

'I'm seeing a psychologist,' I say.

'Still,' he says, as though he's made his point.

'Still, sometimes I get sad,' I say, meeting his gaze. 'And that's okay.'

'It's not just okay, it's bloody natural,' he says, laughing. 'Enough of the crazy-crazy. You're perfectly normal. A bit odd. But then, I'm also a bit odd sometimes.'

'We'll call it even,' I say, and he lets out a mock theatrical groan, hand raised to his forehead. We both begin to chuckle, and I know I will remember this day, and the way in which his laughter fills the room.

# It's Never Too Late

It's an overcast Sunday when the in-laws mind Noah and we head to Karrakatta cemetery to go see Jeremy. Annaya volunteers to drive, and we don't talk much on the way. Despite recent EMDR sessions, I've stayed fundamentally stuck on Jeremy's short life and the years leading up to his death. Jeremy did everything right. He trained obsessively, he was the fastest runner at school, was a solid cricketer and footballer and a strong, good-looking guy. To the majority of us, he was our spirit animal: This, boys, is what a man looks like. He feels no pain, he captains the footy team, and when he hits the punching bag, the walls shake.

Only he wasn't strong. Or maybe he was strong in a perennially broken system that taught boys to numb their pain and to see their feelings as enemies.

We park at the cemetery, walking slowly up to the front office, which sits nestled on the side. We enter the room, and the receptionist motions us over.

'Jeremy Cole,' I say. 'He died in nineteen ninety-seven.'

She types on the computer. Makes a face. Types it again and looks apologetic. 'He's not here,' she says. 'They took him home on the day of the funeral.'

'Oh, okay,' I say, feeling more than a little silly. All those times I had wanted to come. The fear of facing his death and its effects on me.

'I'm sorry,' she says.

'It's okay,' I say, forcing a smile. 'It happens.'

She nods.

'He was a good guy,' I say, apropos of nothing, and we walk out of the office.

Annaya asks if I want to walk around the cemetery for a bit, we're here after all, and so we walk, reading the headstones of strangers.

I stop in front of one Percy Tompkins, 1926 to 2004.

Guy was old, I think. I hope I make it to seventy-eight.

'Do you want to say goodbye?' says Annaya.

'What, here?'

She nods.

'I'm not sure Percy Tompkins would be over the moon about that.'

'He doesn't mind,' she says.

'What, he doesn't mind that some doofus is saying goodbye to a different person in front of his headstone?'

She laughs. 'Well, you need to say goodbye, right?'

'Dear Percy,' I say, in an as literary voice as I can muster. 'You don't know me, but you have a lovely gravestone, and here seems as good a place as any to say goodbye to my friend Jeremy, who is definitely not you.'

'All right,' she says. I keep talking, stressing the importance of Percy Tompkins in my life and how he's gone, but not forgotten. She says, 'Eff off,' takes my hand, and together, we walk on.

It's clear we won't get closure at Karrakatta, so I ask if she can drive us to our old football ground. I tell Annaya it will be suitably solemn. I'll sit on the old steps, imagining us as boys playing on that field.

When we pull in, the carpark is near-full. Walking to the oval, we hear a bugle's cavalry charge two, three times. Turning the corner, the old steps are packed and there's a baseball game in full swing.

'You want to go?'

'No, it's cool,' I say. 'Maybe someone hit a home run or something.'

No one hit a home run. It turns out they celebrate everything in baseball games, like a bunt, or an out, or someone scratching their balls. They do this by playing punk-pop from the early 2000s. They also sound the bugle call each time a person comes to bat, an underwhelming 'Charge' called out by the twenty or so people in attendance. I'm doing okay with the bugle bursts until someone hits a home run and I'm subjected to Good Charlotte's 'I Don't Wanna Be in Love' blaring out of the speakers for the entirety of the batter's lap around the diamond.

Fight or flight kicks in and my pulse begins to race.

'I need to go,' I tell Annaya. 'I want to go, now.'

While I desperately want to leave, I still haven't said goodbye to Jeremy, so we conquer the crest on foot and walk to the adjoining park. Unlike the footy ground, it is a magical flat expanse, two ovals side-by-side.

'This'll do,' I say. 'We played cricket here.'

I sit, silent.

The music from the baseball game's now far enough away so as not to be too distracting. The oval is as I remember it from our days playing cricket, and from high school.

'What are you thinking about?' says Annaya.

The time we found some slides of a naked lady in the bins. The inimitable gut of the president, Daz Warren, in those zip-up Adidas jackets. Eric Coleman running off the pitch, mid-innings, yelling, 'I need to go to the toilet!'

Jeremy bowling like the wind. Or catching the uncatchable. Half the team coming in for the celebration, West Indies style, all high-fives and trick handshakes.

Sleepovers at Jeremy's, in the midst of my parents splitting. Hoping there was a Wildcats or a West Coast Eagles match we could see. Nothing on at all, so we watched *Hitchcock's Rope* instead, laughing at how silly and staged it all felt.

'*Lethal Weapon*, man, that's a movie,' said Jeremy.

I watched it, years later. It wasn't great to think about why Jeremy identified with Riggs, but I guess that didn't matter anymore.

The feeling I'd be fine as long as I had a friend like him. Stayovers in high school too. We'd talk about the girls we liked, say hey, maybe our kids will get to play together, when we're married and stuff.

'Just thinking about Jeremy,' I say. 'I miss him.'

'I know.'

The last time I saw him was at Steve's bar in Nedlands, just after his eighteenth birthday. I was so stoked to bump into him. He was happy to see me too. We grabbed a beer, sat at the bar, and caught up, quick speed. Soon enough it was time to go. A quick hand-slap of a shake and then out.

I didn't know it would be the last time I'd get to see him. If I had known, I would have held the shake a little longer, maybe pulled him in for a hug. But I didn't, and now it's much too significant – simply my last moment with him still alive, and so I replay it over and over, to spend one second more with him, only this time I say, 'Hey, Jeremy, don't go, mate. Just stay for a bit.'

After a while, the sun slides behind the clouds and the cold kicks in. I squeeze Annaya's hand. 'Shall we go?'

'Are you okay?'

'I'm good,' I say. 'Come on, let's go home.'

I hope one day I'll find a way to honour his life, and maybe this is it: some words I found to honour a friend, gone too soon, lost to me but never forgotten.

# Role Play

In September 2015, weeks prior to my ankle operation, I officially graduate from The University of Western Australia. My father and Annaya come to the ceremony, with my in-laws looking after Noah. Annaya regularly checks her phone in case something's happened with our boy in the hour so since we left. My father wears a suit and wraparound sunglasses that are too big for his face, and jokes with security guards about 'joining the team'.

We don't stay long. You rarely do in early parenthood. I eat a spring roll and a triangle of egg sandwich and then it's time to go pick up Noah. When we get home, Annaya gives me a card, a blue badge fastened to that says *You did it!* in thick yellow letters.

Completing my PhD brings up an array of emotions. Firstly, I feel relieved to have completed it, Secondly, I feel a sense of disappointment, not so much with the project itself, but because I'm burdened by my now upended life, living as a dad and a writer, all while still carefully monitoring my father's recovery and increasing concerns over Trent, whose struggles with addiction are threatening to sink him once and for all.

Dad says at the graduation that Trent is doing okay, no job, but there's nothing silly going on, and perhaps that's more worrying. That, in the years since rock bottom, his being unemployed is better than him being somewhere where they lock your cell, or they build another fence, because, as Trent so beautifully put it, 'They don't want us to see the trees.'

And then, while I'm dealing with that, it's time to go in for my ankle reconstruction.

The surgery itself is uneventful, although my specialist is *furious* that I drank a glass of water. From there we go in and he gets the job done.

Soon after, I'm back home, and for twelve weeks I wear a moon boot and ride around on a knee walker. Noah's obsessed with the walker. In time, we make it a game, where I race around the house, fall over a little too much and Noah bursts out laughing every time.

Throughout this period, my father-in-law is omnipresent. We've moved out of our apartment and are now living in the house of my brother-in-law Arshan, which has been recently purchased but is not yet inhabited, as he's waiting for his fiancé to come over from India. The in-laws live five houses down so it's close enough for a walk-in, which they do often, grateful for the proximity to their beloved daughter and grandson.

While I'm incapacitated, my father-in-law, Dinyar, speaks often about what I'll do post-PhD. Arshan is already in state government. 'Good prospects,' he says. He doesn't add, 'Unlike, say, if you've done a PhD in Creative Writing,' but it's implied. That's okay, as for me, writing has never been a choice. Or if it is, it's a choice made in the same way that I chose to have a child: it seemed the best way for me to move on and have a happy and fulfilling life.

Conversations with my father-in-law are alarmingly frank, all held at our dining table, as Noah bounces a ball on the tiles, spills a drink or jumps up for an impromptu cuddle, nearly reinjuring my leg in the process.

Dinyar tells me about his time working, supporting his family of ten kids. I do the math and consider how we're struggling with *one*. Are we doing a good job? I don't know. Are we earning enough money? Again, I don't know.

In the end, I'm swayed by constant chats about wages and responsibility. We talk through my job options, and it's mostly web stuff. Annaya's searching for me too, and eventually, she finds a job that might work. A six-month contract in government. I head to the website, see a picture of a giant machine cog against red dirt, black text on a white background and think, *Geez, that's some pretty dry content there.*

Trent calls me on an otherwise forgettable Friday afternoon. From the first word, his voice and style of speech are different yet depressingly familiar. He needs money, and that's fine, I can and have previously handled that for him. Sometimes it went to something concrete, but as far as I could tell, it mostly just evaporated.

Trent only immediately needs money for certain things during certain phases of his life, and this seems to be one of those phases, and is the first I've known about since Noah's birth.

I can't deal with it anymore. I'm nearly forty, and he's three years older than me. I yell at him over the phone, knowing all the while he's not listening. He tells me it's hard for him, and I believe that, only it's hard for all kinds of people for all kinds of reasons, and yet they don't all drop out of life, expecting someone else to foot the bill.

I think to myself, *Mate, you're being pretty harsh*. But that's me now. I'm a dad, and one whose job is, or should be, to protect and look after my kids. Before this, my brother's choices were annoying and often frustrating. Now that I have Noah, they're just dangerous.

As we end the call, I know he's most likely not coming back this time. It seems that really, this is less a phase and more the beginning of a slow, steady decline.

'It really gets to you, doesn't it?' says Annaya, and I nod, knowing on one level I've failed him and that I also no longer have the time or the energy to help him.

In years past, I just mucked in, over and over. Only nothing ever changed, and we're not kids anymore. How long can you keep making the same mistakes and expecting others to get you out of them?

Even so, while I was dressing down my brother for being irresponsible, I realised I'd be doing the same if I didn't take this job, and a chance to provide for my family. In Trent's freefall, I saw the possibility for a twist of fate to send me into a similar crisis.

Every desperate word of his highlighted the potential for a wrong choice of mine to damage me or my family.

So, I do it. I take the government job, and a short-term contract, so I can bring home the bacon. There are no prospects, perks, or social programs of note at the workplace. I'll just be doing the work, that thing a man is supposed to do, however he is feeling, and whatever he really wants to do.

# CONNECTION

## The Right Thing

Somewhat predictably, I'm anxious about starting my new job. I'm scared I won't fit in. The content seems dull, and I'll have to commute into the city. Another part of me knows that any change, good or bad, typically provokes this anxiety response in me. So, I decide to give this job a go and to at least see if I'm right about my fears in this instance.

My work, by the way, is as a web content coordinator. Someone comes to me if they want to put content on the website. I then go one of the heads of department with the content in a Word-formatted document for them to sign off on, which they sometimes do in an hour and sometimes over the course of three weeks. From there, I go to the next head of department. And then, after the document has been signed off by various parties, sometimes up to the level of the Director General, and provided the content is still current – which is not always the case – I put it online, a task that would otherwise take an hour, tops.

It's boring work caught up in unnecessary hoops of clearance, where everything you do has a one-hundred-page manual, only there's no point reading past point five because that's when they tell you to bring together some sort of CHOGM-style delegation to sign off on a release that authorises the changing of 'i-Phone' to 'iPhone'.

My inner critic asks me what I'm doing. It says, *What part of keep going don't you get?*

I say I'm in a family again, and again I'm feeling pressure to survive.

*No one knows you better than you*, it says. *Why not just go after what you really want?*

As is sometimes the case, here my inner critic makes a good point.

My father-in-law's take on the subject, however, is particularly clear. You have a baby now. You have no time anymore to write in research forests or eat banitsa on the Black Sea Coast. You now have roles and responsibilities. You need to stick at this real job so you can start to be a real dad.

I buy some dress pants and some shirts that say *I'm here to work, not to party*. My boss, Amy, greets me on the first day, and walks me over to a desk in a different area to hers, and which is around the corner from my other colleague in the comms team. Having found my spot, I begin my work, touching base with various heads of department to check currency and accuracy of information and making sure the links through to all related department assets and information sheets are still functioning.

Amy's on leave for the second day, and on that day, I'm harassed by a person at a higher paygrade than mine to attend a meeting, immediately, and without my manager around to take part in proceedings.

When Amy returns the next week, we head to HR. The HR officer is apologetic but already seems defeated. I'm told later they have a file on this employee with a number of similar complaints. No one ever mentions why nothing has ever been done about them.

I ask a colleague if we can go get a coffee. I tell her I already feel invisible within the greater structure of our department. While she's sympathetic, she's heard story after story like this, powerless people grasping for the smallest ounce of control in jobs they don't particularly enjoy. Some learn to adapt to it, some transcend it through the things they do out of working hours, and a great deal more find better paid, more purposeful work that better plays to their strengths.

I come home deflated and say, 'I hate this job.'

'But you've just started,' Annaya says.

I tell my father-in-law that it's not a great fit for my particular skillset.

'But there are good prospects,' he says.

Which is fine, only all the while, I'm falling into depression.

I talk less to Noah most nights, even though he's now three years old, and fast developing a greater grasp of the intricacies of the English language. I talk less to Annaya too, because who wants to talk after days like that? Who wants to revel in nature, or play Uno when it's all you can do to get out of bed in the morning?

I gain a lot of weight and have to head to Johnny Bigg for 3XL and 4XL clothing. Over time, the morning traffic starts to get me down, and the parking is expensive, although at that point it's still close to the building.

Over the coming months, they start building on my original carpark, and so I pay more and park farther away. To get to work from there, you have to walk through a previously busy, thriving plaza that's now a ghost town barring the single cafe that remains among the red brick walls, and empty storefronts.

Over time, people get new jobs in better government departments, which results in a mad scramble for their offices if they were in management, or for the right to use their cubicle as storage if they were one of the plebs.

Over time, a married guy starts fucking a married girl and fellow workmate, and eventually they find a new, more liberated life together. Another guy has split up from his wife and sleeps overnight in the sick bay. One lady's often drunk and another keeps acting like we're in The White House. She barks comments at her colleagues, and at times I'm half-expecting her to yell, 'Come on, boffins!' like Raymond Terrific from Big Talk.

All that time, I continue to do 'the right thing'. I get in early and leave late. For months and months, I'm the first one there at morning teas; I say hello and wave goodbye. I do things correctly, or as correctly as I can.

And all the while, I feel like I am dying.

So what exactly is so ill-fitting about this job for me, as opposed to anyone else in that same role?

I would say *everything*, but that's hiding the real issue. As far I can tell, this job won't work for me because I no longer know how to switch 'me' off. For many years before my PhD, I'd get out of bed by pretending that caring about boring stuff and not caring about writing was manageable. In truth, it was greatly dispiriting, and each day required a herculean effort on my part to stay motivated given I already knew what I wanted to do with my life, and was doing something else.

To put that into perspective, I found my calling at the age of twenty-five. From that point, I was willing to do anything to make that calling my life and my job, whatever the consequences to my social life, my bank balance, or my ability to secure a mortgage. Somehow, while working all manner of other mind-numbingly crap jobs, I actually pulled it off and made a profession out of my acquired knowledge and increased skills in the area of creative writing.

It's a conversation I have often with Annaya after my PhD. I say, 'Angel, there's no way this is going to work. I can't just push down all I am for the sake of a pay cheque.'

'She says, 'We need the money.' She says this despite the fact that we're both working part-time, and parenting full-time, and already exhausted. Heck, I'm not even sure there's a win for us in any of our potential scenarios. And so eventually, I see that in this situation we're both right, and both up against all kinds of external stresses, so we'll need to do something to get out of this stalemate.

In the land of government work, I'm quiet, though occasionally I come to life in front of the odd kind soul, or firefly of a workmate. Mostly, though, I follow protocols, I tick boxes, and I update web content with the efficiency of a lobotomised robot.

I write up Content Update Authorisation forms and leave them in people's trays or pass them on to their PAs. I archive old content because the site is running like a 1978 Datsun, and I need to do something to speed it up. I talk to the people in the cubicles around me in the hope that someone does something much more interesting than this when they're not at work.

There's Gordon, who used to be in a rock band, still plays music, and who's generally a joy to be around. He's getting on – but aren't we all? – so I ask him what it was like to be famous, and he says it was good for a bit, but only a precious few get to make a living from their art.

My teammate Tess has long blonde hair and has been told on more than one occasion that she looks like Elsa from *Frozen*. She talks mostly about her kids, and that's cool because you can see the love in her eyes whenever she does this. When you're talking with her about things that aren't work – and that could be art, food, anything really – she comes to life as if you've flicked a switch. I like that I can make her laugh. I also like that our main job seems to be keeping each other sane in this otherwise batshit enterprise.

The drive is tough, with lines of cars headed into the city on the Mitchell Freeway, backed up from Ocean Reef Road, still more than twenty kilometres away from our destination. Commutes turn into slow progressions, inching forward, bit by bit, headed to somewhere I'd rather not be in the first place.

Over time, the parking pay machines start malfunctioning in the new carpark, so I have to put my ticket in exactly the right way.

In time, the carpark undercroft starts leaking, and the escalators stop working, and they start to scaffold all around the building.

Over time they begin works on the Mitchell Freeway, and that extends my trip, giving me closer to an hour to consider why I'm doing this job and how much of my soul I still have left to give.

In mid-2016, a year after I was selected for the job, they move me out of my team of three and into a team of two, with Tess in an office and me in a cubicle. While I don't see my harasser anymore, I don't see anyone else either. My boss gives me another twelve-month contract and then leaves for a better role in a different department. In her place they put someone who's already terrified of losing their job.

Some people are let go. Some new people are hired, and some of them are also let go. Teams become mega-teams, taking on other teams' work until it's not so much a team as a hodgepodge of irritable people who remember what things used to be like when the department was better resourced. They talk of people long gone. They tell the stories of the cubicles, the projects and the teams (oh, the teams!) as though they're no longer in the same office space. They say, 'That's when it was the Department of Futures,' or 'Remember when we were Assessment and Analysis Services?'

I become really good, like Olympic level, at taking toilet breaks, and walks, sometimes out of the building and into the surrounding parklands. It's on one of these walks that I see my boss's boss stood high up on the overpass, watching cars go by.

He smiles when he sees me. Says, 'You alright?'

And I nod, because it's better than saying, *This job is the drizzling shits.*

Over time, it gets to me – all these things are *done*, although they never explain why. I do them anyway and wonder if, when all this is done, I will remember my earlier dreams of creativity, community and connection.

## Like Stones

While our time raising Noah is challenging, soon enough Annaya and I start talking about having another baby. Our plan was always to have two: Annaya has read that three years is the perfect gap between siblings, so now is the time.

I'm nervous about having two kids, given Noah is already a high-needs child, and given Annaya's previous experience with postnatal depression and mine with postnatal anxiety. After much discussion, though, we agree another child might be just what Noah needs; someone to focus on other than himself and in time, a beloved sibling.

Just prior to Noah's third birthday in September 2016, Annaya falls pregnant. The thought of a second child brings a small, quiet joy alongside pre-existing sadness. We don't care if it's a boy or a girl, we simply hope it's happy and healthy. We walk into the spare room and imagine what it will be like to have another child. We go back to Baby Bunting, tossing up between a nappy bin with baking soda or a new change table.

Annaya smiles a nervous smile, one you only see in mums, as they not only know those first few weeks can be risky but also feel the burden of responsibility if anything were to go wrong. It's the strangest, cruellest thing – you're told nothing's locked in until the sixteen-week mark.

We go to the six-week appointment, waiting patiently in

reception. Once in, they rub jelly on her stomach and search for a baby.

The operator rubs and moves. Pauses, moves the monitor, rubs again over her belly. She finds *something*, more a smudge than a bub and says, 'I think that's it.'

Only it's not. We all know what a baby looks like. In the end, she says, 'It's inconclusive.' She's not congratulatory, more apologetic. And so, we drive home thinking, *This cannot be good.*

Within a couple of weeks, Annaya has a heavy bleed. I find her in bed, crying on a Saturday night, after coming home from a work dinner. I get in and hug her, and we don't sleep until late that night. We're stuck thinking we had something, but knowing we didn't, or we did but we no longer do. It's just me and Annaya, grateful for our first child but still grieving what we have lost.

The more we talk to other parents, the more we learn how common miscarriages are, both for women trying to have their first children, and those trying to conceive after a prior successful pregnancy. A friend mentions his wife having recently gone through a miscarriage. He does this as quickly as possible. It needs acknowledgement, and yet there's nothing to be done after that point. It's not something you move past. It's something that forever changes you forever, even if, in time, it's more a room inside of you as opposed to the whole house.

When I'm not working at my government job, I assess manuscripts. When I'm not doing that, I put Noah to bed, nearly nodding off as I'm doing it. It's as if my only way out of this grief is to not feel things, to close it all off and get on with it.

I carry on until one day, I'm in Sydney, for a launch of a book I edited. I love Sydney and always have, only this time it feels too loud, and much too busy.

I arrive in Glebe much too early for the launch. Walking down Glebe Point Road, I can't stop thinking about Annaya and the baby we lost. I walk into a new-age store and ask the shop assistant, Vyan, for a stone to help my wife with her grief. I hold up a heart-shaped one I've found. He tells me that one is not for the type of pain we are currently facing.

He starts to tell me about the different kinds of crystals. I say I'm not sure I can stay here much longer. I'm not feeling great, and I'm scared that I won't cope if he keeps talking about crystals.

He nods after my admission, says, 'Oh,' as though I've asked him for a different colour crystal. He walks from behind the counter and guides me to a corner of the store, which, if I am being honest, looks exactly like the rest of it.

Vyan finds me a special stone. He tells me about it, but really, it's noise. He keeps going, stressing the positive qualities of the stone, the ways in which it opens up the grief and heals the heart.

'These things, you need to feel them,' he says, and I nod, although I tell myself that this will never happen.

I thank him, feeling sick at the sight of the pebble in my

hand. It's tiny, a full stop to something that seems to have no end; too small to do anything but mock our loss. We go back to the counter and Vyan wraps the crystal. He makes me wait a bit, talks me through the cleaning of the stone. I nod but no longer look at him, practically begging him to hand me the bag.

I leave, walk quickly to Victoria Park. Unwrap the stone. Hold it in my palm and want only to ditch it in the lake. Sitting in this often beautiful, always welcoming city, I wonder if I should walk into the depths of the pond and sink slowly beneath the water.

On my way back up Glebe Point Road to head back to Gleebooks, where I'm launching the book, I feel a hand on my shoulder. It's Vyan, wide-eyed and nervous.

He's made up two bags of stones: one for Annaya and one for me, as he saw how much I was hurting. He tells me the story behind each stone and why he chose it. It's clear he did this as soon as I had left and had waited, watching, in the hope he could help.

He waits, expectantly. Eventually, I well up. I don't know what to think or say. In the end, he hands over the bags. He goes to leave, then says, 'Hey man, I took a big risk doing this. Can I please have a hug?'

I nod, and then we hug like brothers. 'Thank you.'

'That's okay.'

'I thought we were going to have another baby.'

'I know,' he says. 'Maybe you will, just not right now.' He smiles and walks back to the shop, so I find a bench in an afterthought of a park next to a shopping centre and then cry for our baby, and for all that we lost.

Upon my return, I go back to my desk, which is now in the library, for reasons I've not yet discovered. They begin another restructure (they're always restructuring) on account of the incoming Labor government, and web content now sits under library services. In my all-too-frequent coffee breaks in my new digs, I wonder why Maxwell House went into coffee when it's clearly not one of their strengths. I look up the org charts, see a blank space on account of a recent death, a man who'd been there longer than I've been alive, and my eyes start to blur.

I get through the days, thanks mostly to the studious, generous and welcoming library staff who seem intent to enjoy my presence, though it's still clear I'm not long for this department. As final months go it's not the worst place to watch one's dreams evaporate, and it's there that I again begin to see the world outside of my current contract. I watch the clock. I talk to my library colleagues about arthouse cinema – I studied and made films for my bachelor's degree – and watch the sun as it sneaks through the far windows each afternoon.

And then one day Annaya again falls pregnant, and not even my impending obsolescence can keep me from enjoying this unforeseen, much appreciated second chance.

Annaya and I don't mention the last time, or talk much aside from practicalities, although we're both scared we'll again lose the baby. We cross our fingers. We pray to gods in whom we've never believed. I talk to Annaya's belly when she lets me. I apologise in advance to the bump that's so quickly forming about my current vocational choices and promise one day soon I will again follow my heart.

I stay excited about the baby. I stay miserable about my job. The idea in all of this seems to be that I, and men by extension, are not meant to enjoy what we do unless what we do is already meaningful in the societal context. Thus a doctor, a geologist, or a dentist can love their work if they want to, but a writer is taking the piss. *The deal if you do you*, they seem to say, *is that you're being selfish, as opposed to being true to yourself.*

My friend Lindy takes a photo of me around this time, at a festival in which we're both featured authors. When I say I've gained weight, I mean I've piled it on. You can't see my eyes, only my cheeks, and dark cave entries where my eyes are supposed to be. It's as if I ate myself, and now there's two of us, with a tiny, lost version of me stuck inside the other's expansive body.

# The Light

Josh is born in July 2017, weighing seven pounds, three ounces. Like his brother, he is a C-section, only this time it's planned under medical advice, as opposed to being an emergency.

This time around we are more comfortable with the journey. We know what's coming, so can prepare for each step.

Josh seems more comfortable too. While in the ultrasounds Noah often looked cradled, even quiet, as he grew, Josh is very much there – his round head bobbing up and down in images, his heart the thunder of galloping horses.

The planned birth of Josh is in the morning. And, while the birth is still a delicate process, the speed of said process is greatly increased, and Annaya's more awake and more able to be present this time as well, and I see how much that means to her from the moment she's holding her bub, and this time doesn't have to immediately let him go.

We prep Noah repeatedly for Josh's arrival, find books that explain what's happening, and how. What the changes mean, and how he will soon become a big brother. In theory, it's to be a special, sacred space. And yet both Noah and I seem to already know we'll miss the two of us, anchored only to each other; lying together at bedtime and counting the stars on his ceiling; mornings where he has the run of my side of the bed, and can snuggle in close without fear of interruption.

The days after the birth I spend my daytimes with Annaya and Josh at the hospital, while my in-laws look after Noah, and then I'm home by five to spend time with Noah, cook dinner, do bath time, and then stories, songs, or any number of ways that I have found to help him drift off to sleep.

That week we often lie together in bed, we go back to staring up at his glow-in-the-dark galaxy. He gets me to name the planets one by one. He asks how they were formed, and how and where they orbit. I tell him all I know, in the knowledge that the constellations are again about to shift.

When Josh comes home, we return to the familiar lack of sleep that we first endured through Noah's early years. When Josh is in a bassinet in our room, his ruptured sleeps are tough. Once he's in his own room, they become even tougher.

For reasons I can never ascertain, Josh saves his non-compliance for bedtime. Thus, when it is time to settle him, the boy I meet with a tender 'hello' is less a newborn and more like a man at a deli who's waited too long for his corned-beef sandwich. We never wonder if Josh is awake – he declares it, loudly, and continues to shout until one or both of us are in there addressing his concerns.

My settle routine, repeated two to three times a night, is usually thus:

- Feel the poke of Annaya's elbow. Let her pokes turn into palm-based shoves and say, 'What's up?'
- Hear the screaming. Assume there's an intruder or

a fire. Ask what time is, like it matters. Never get an answer from Annaya and so go to settle Josh, all the while secretly furious she woke me up to get the baby. Never consider the possibility she has got him three times already and so desperately needs the sleep. Also never consider the possibility that parenting is, well, doing things you don't really want to do.

- Bustle through the house and reach the cot. Try to talk through the issue with Josh like it's a hostage negotiation, a series of repetitions of 'what's wrong?' met with louder cries until I scoop him into my arms.
- Soothing singing of 'Eternal Flame' by The Bangles, during which Josh begins to settle. At that moment, I feel strangely calm, almost serene, and we dance in the dark until I'm sure he has fallen asleep.

The colic and associated restless sleep Noah encountered are distant memories with Josh, though he does seem more dependent on proximity and touch. That's natural, of course, but that doesn't stop my arms hurting, or me wondering how to take a wee with a newborn in my arms. It's also tougher to balance my work and home life as I only have two weeks leave for Josh's birth, whereas with Noah I was able to take six months off from my PhD.

Noah loves Josh immediately. He hugs him on the couch, kisses his head. Josh is equally in awe of Noah. In one of my favourite pictures, the three of us are squeezed into a selfie,

Noah's grin as wide as the sky, with Josh gazing up in wonder at this smiley, ebullient kid. In another, they're both in Josh's cot, the elder boy grinning, the younger not yet quite sure what their bond is and why.

Days alone with Josh come more rarely than they did with Noah but are just as precious. He rocks a wide brim hat like a boss, loves parks, loves me. It's rare to find a photo where he's not filling the frame. It's even rarer to find one where he's not chomping down on some kind of sweet treat.

And when he smiles – my god, that smile. So bereft of worry and so filled with an abundance of contentment.

He's soon the glue of our family. It's unexpected, as a baby can be disruptive at the best of times. In Noah's case, he came midway through my PhD, only weeks after my father fell into a coma. By contrast, Josh shows up at a point of culmination. Things are calmer, more controlled. We know what we're doing. Dad's worked through his rehab and is getting back to speed, and sits quietly with Josh in his arms, as if to say, 'What do you mean? Have I not been here the whole time?'

My mother, freed by not needing to save us, shows up this time as a VIP. I work through the week, but we enjoy spring days out back on the weekend, with a shifting sun poking through the palms. Morning coffees at Avoka, an open indoor space with plants on the walls and room to move, with Josh clad in a beanie, my mum taking time to hold him, the two of them, eyes locked on each other, with matching smiles.

Annaya's parents have also seemed to exhale a sigh of relief.

Well suited to a newborn, they were beginning to struggle with the needs of an increasingly older boy with an insatiable need for physical activity.

A friend of mine has not been able to have kids. He visits, holds my baby boy as if it is his own. Noah gets time with me and his mum, not usually at the same time, but even that time seems to buoy him. The focus has shifted, and this in turns means he is not so worried, as if maybe there's a weight that has come off him because he is no longer the sole focus of our concern.

What kind of problems do we face? Exhaustion. Money. Job satisfaction. Juggling one's old life and one's new life and struggling to find balance. Is it hard to raise a child? Incredibly so. It's harder still to raise two, which we find out in due course, but there is still so much solace in those early days. The way a newborn nestles into your shoulder, a cuddly, soft, sweet-smelling accessory that goes with everything. The realisation that your elder child is growing too and falling in love with all they've already become.

There aren't too many talks between Annaya and me: there's no time. For the most part, it's a reunion, a bringing together of the folks who helped us raise our first child. And, while Dad's different since his accident, there is so much of him that still remains, and the parts that have changed seem almost for the better.

And strangely, just as Josh arrives, my book and PhD project is scheduled for publication. *You Belong Here* is about how the kids of a divorce come together to break generational dysfunction. It's a tough read in parts, in part because while it's not literally true, it's emotionally true that for my family, my parents' divorce hurt us all, with aftershocks felt for years to come.

It's not lost on me that by the book's end, there is also a glimmer of hope. And yet, that hope comes not from those who went through the trauma. It comes from the first child of the next generation after them. Through her eyes, there's the possibility we can leave the pain and intergenerational trauma behind and move into a place of light, love and forgiveness.

## You Belong Here

In February 2018, the culmination of eight years of writing, both before, during and after my PhD reaches its apex with the publication of my debut novel, *You Belong Here*. Between the time I start researching the work and when I complete the work, I survive on the scent of single-story publications, occasional prizes and some reflective non-fiction, so I can continue to say I exist as a writer.

None of that is easy. I find pockets of time to write late at night and am often interrupted by Josh waking even as I start to get going. After I resettle him, I go again. A lot of what I write in this time is fragmented at best, and likely feeds into my next project, a collection of short fiction set in Perth and regional Western Australia.

With my first novel now accepted for publication, it's a happy time. We head down south to Margaret River, stay at a family resort, and aside from a particularly foolish swimming teacher on vacation telling my water-nervous, not yet swimming boy to 'just jump in', we ride the waves impressively given our youngest is only six months old and has to share a room with his older brother.

I tell my publisher I want to write a note in the front of every pre-order. I enjoy writing the notes immensely. However, there's also something of the people-pleaser in that act. It's almost an apology, as though my book was never going to be enough without including a personal, heartfelt note of thanks.

My publisher is already starting to tire of the exertion required to launch a book with this adaptative, can-do me. She tells me writers feel entitled. For me, it's not entitlement. I put everything I had into making it as a writer for fifteen years in a space where almost everything else had to take a back seat, and now all I can see is how my moment might be ruined, or the ways in which my journey with this book won't be enough to make up for all the sacrifices made in pursuit of this goal.

Things do not start particularly well. At my first event at a writer's festival, they give me a tiny room, perhaps having assumed I was not much of a drawcard. The line is down the hall when I arrive. We head inside and the room's already full. The festival allowed patrons to stay in from a previous session, and with me being a local writer, many oblige. Outside, there are frantic discussions I'm not privy to: Mum, Dad, Annaya and Eve are eventually let in. My best friend is not, and neither are many other good friends.

At the signing table after the event, some friends head down and tell me they'd been turned away. Others tell me the bookstore is already out of stock. This nearly breaks me, in that it feels like neither the festival nor my publisher have the same level of faith I have in my book.

I ask my publisher if we can have another event, a launch

in the city, to include the many people who didn't get to see my festival event, and she generously agrees. This time things click. Soon after that, my favourite bookstore in Perth invites me to do an in-conversation. During these events, and in the embraces of friends and family, things feel like they might actually be okay. Perhaps in those moments they are, and I just placed so much hope, and increased expectation on my debut novel needing to be a whole house, as opposed to the front gate in my literary career.

Soon after that, I begin to accumulate the various blog posts, comments and social media shares for a later post to say thank you for the support and kind words. In such a space, and with so many smiles on the faces of friends as they hold my book aloft, or read it on a beach, or single out a particular paragraph that they loved, it becomes increasingly hard to feel put out by the natural ups and downs of a debut author's journey. As the feelings, sometimes joyous and sometimes disappointed, arrive in waves, I see that there's an opportunity with this book and a way to distinguish what matters to my soul, that is quite separate from any notions of success and achievement.

In June of that year Trent Dalton spoils a party that, if I'm being honest, had barely started, with the release of his debut novel, *Boy Swallows Universe*, and I struggle to process that disparity of scale. I'm not sure whether it's fair to compare his journey to mine. On some level, though, that's how I'd wanted my book to be seen: as strong, striking, an exciting new name in Australian literature.

Soon after that, I'm thrust into a lifestyle festival, via an email request sent to my publisher. We set up a schedule for my appearance in an afternoon session, and things seem to be okay. I ask about the appearance fee via email and things go frosty.

'There's no appearance fee,' writes one of the organisers in response. 'I think something has not been communicated.'

It's clear that I am meant to be grateful for the opportunity. And so, as a man of my word, I agree to appear at the event.

In their correspondence, they tell me not to park in the main carpark, as it will be flat-out. And so, on the afternoon of my event, I drive to the venue, past a ghostly main carpark and start to worry if there's anyone here at all, before heading out to where they told me to park, where, coincidentally, there are no other cars. Once in the building, I head to the main foyer where a woman stands, mobile phone in hand.

'I'm Laurie Steed, I'm here for a panel.'

She swipes at her phone, scrolling quickly through a list of names. 'Well, you're not on the list.'

'I can go,' I say, my feet almost skidding on the concrete as I turn to depart.

'No, no, you're not getting away that easy,' she says and picks up the program.

Once we reach my photo, I say, 'That's me.'

She says, 'That's not you.'

I do the same face as in the picture, and she says, 'Oh, it is you.' She straps a fluoro green band on my wrist – I don't know what it's for, and she doesn't tell me.

In my head, I thought I was attending a writers festival. Once inside the main hall, however, I see stall after stall: wheatgrass, reiki, the power of coloured tubes, people who massage your sit bones, aura cleansers, and the wonder of those weird head scratcher things that were big in the nineties.

A sign points upstairs, the word 'conversations' written in blue marker, surrounded by a rainbow of colour. Once upstairs, I find one of the organisers.

'Hi, I'm Laurie.'

'Oh, hello,' they say, meeting my gaze, but then turning back to survey the expo floor. 'Quite the crowd we have booked in.'

'Really?' I say. I'm not sure how that could possibly be true as there were twenty-five cars in the carpark, tops.

'A couple of buses coming in,' they say, 'So head on through. Enjoy your session!'

Inside, beyond the double doors, there are three people on the stage and three in the audience. As we get closer to the start time, a handful of people come in. I sit down, introduce myself to the other panellists. It's a fascinating mix of writers, psychologists, and one dude I still can't get my head around.

We begin, with the five of us (four panellists plus the host) sitting as if set up for a firing line, holding corded mics, with our fluoro green bands glowing on our wrists. What follows turns out to be a pretty good conversation, as facilitated by an enthusiastic, energetic host.

It's just a shame there wasn't anyone to see it. Indeed, I'd love to tell you what the audience thought, but I counted more people last time I visited the urinals at my local shopping centre.

I leave immediately after the event, pacing past the main carpark, before jogging back to the car. I drive home the long way, down the coast, only nothing's on the radio, and I'm not sure why we can't play something on commercial FM radio other than 'The Horses', or 'Run To Paradise'.

I knew my dream of publication might differ from reality. Even so, I'm still surprised by how it feels, and the waves of emotion that wash over me in the months after my book is published. I mean, Christ, it took me eight years to write this book. I had hoped to write a novel about people, rather than characters. A family love story that was raw, real and vulnerable.

I really thought that I had done that.

I come home that day, get through dinner, baths and into the bedtime routine. I cuddle Noah in his bed as he reads, push my face into the back of his hoodie, close my eyes.

'Dad, you're squeezing me,' he says.

'Sorry.'

'How was your day?'

'I did an event.'

He smiles. 'Was it good?'

'No.'

'Did you belong there?' he says, his grin growing wider.

'I hope not. If I do, then we are totally screwed.'

'We are in deep ca-ca,' says Noah, and bursts out laughing, and I laugh too, and then lean in for the tickle. He writhes like an eel but comes back with his own attack, and I go 'argh!' and then he falls back and sighs once his laughter subsides.

# SIGNIFICANT OTHERS

## Teambuilding

In March 2019, my contract ends at the government job. It's there that I realise I'm debating communication protocols while my youngest son is taking his first steps. I'm drinking my fourth coffee of the day, stuck in a meeting that's going nowhere, as my eldest receives his merit certificate.

Am I good at my work? Well, sure, but I'm also quite good at digging a ditch, and you don't see me doing that. Which is not to say there's no merit in providing for your family. It's more that the most common thing I find when talking to people here is that they're not all that committed to their work. This is doubly the case with the men I meet. Perhaps there's a method to that madness, and a way to keep them well away from emotional intimacy. I can tell you one thing, though: in nearly three years at the job I rarely, if ever, have a conversation with a man about anything other than work, the footy, or what time we'll knock off.

When I finish the job, I want to shout, 'I made it!' from the rooftops, only there are more pressing things on my mind. I'm desperate to write, but also prepared for well-meaning but dismissive conversations about how I need to find a new job, rather than obsessing about this pipedream of mine. I've secured funding to write my next book – in no small part thanks to the support and guidance of Lara, a friend, colleague, and career catalyst, with whom I share a no-money-exchanged, skillshare relationship – so I can say I am a real writer. At the same time, I also feel a great deal of pressure to get this book right, because if I don't, then my choice will see a direct impact on the family budget.

At first, story after story, not unlike those I wrote in earlier years, come flooding out. I feel a rush writing them that's unparalleled. It also feels like I'm honouring a gift from a friend and fellow writer during a trip to Varuna when she said, 'Why be the next Dave Eggers when you could be the first Laurie Steed?'

At this point, Josh, previously locked into a regular sleep cycle, again begins to wake at absurd hours. Initially, I'll wake startled and a little frustrated, an initial 'Buddy … ' giving way to a pick-up cuddle and a kiss on his head. If I'm desperate, and it is clear he's not already super drowsy, a song or two often gets him off to sleep. We've now moved on to 'Dream a Little Dream', and 'Can't Take My Eyes Off You'. How did I come up with those songs? I have no idea. While I've always loved the bombast of that *da da, da da, da da DA da da* bridge in the latter, they're otherwise songs that I think of roughly once every seven years. Why do they work? Well, I guess because the sentiment is surprisingly apt for when you're holding a newborn in your arms. You love them, you want them to have sweet dreams, and apart from that, the rest is just noise.

Over time, getting up with Josh becomes a ritual of its own. Sometimes, I wonder if he's not soothing me as much as I am soothing him. Still, I'm so tired. Indeed, I can't think of another time when I was this tired, day after day, and year after year before we had kids.

These nights with Josh, and the themes they encapsulate, eventually bleed into my story collection, *Greater City Shadows*, creating a conflict between the man I've been and the one I'm becoming. Gone are the musings of lone protagonists as they gaze out at empty fields, or struggle like Gatsby's boats, forever beating on against the present and so often carried back to their past. In their place are stories of tired, devoted dads, and extended families rallying around to ease the demands of early parenting.

The more that I work from home, the more the blurring of life and work becomes a noticeable issue. It feels as though I'm particularly struggling as a parent, which will likely mean the need to prioritise the family over my writing for a bit.

Annaya's struggling too. Her worry braid, which rests off the side of her face, first twisted into being during the early years of Noah, is now closer to a dreadlock. Again, we're tired, and again we're stressed, and it's not uncommon for me to be writing, with headphones in, on the couch, and for her to be in bed, with her iPad on her knees, and her phone in her hand.

In life, Josh spills his drink, or Noah breaks a plate, and they need me, period. That need doesn't dissipate by my being 'at work' because physically, I'm still inside the family home.

In such times, I'm often interrupted from an important phone call by a naked Noah shouting as he streaks past the glass-panel door to my office. When Josh knocks gently on that same door, I can't just yell, 'Go away,' because I'm stressed or tired, or unsure of when my next contract or funding opportunity will show up.

Noah haphazardly pushes the buttons on my printer and Josh knocks over my coffee cup, and as they both bounce on my reading chair, I'm supposed to let it go. It's not easy to do this, and it's only when Noah takes my first edition of *A Movable Feast* and tears the dust jacket in two that I reluctantly ask Annaya to take the kids for a bit.

Annaya works too, three days a week, although I greatly envy her ability to go to an office away from the home on those days (which is ironic, given all those months I too was working away from home and hating the experience). I suggest my renting a space and she says, 'How, exactly, are we going to pay for that?'

Most conversations come back to money. My writing and writing-related activities often earn less than her job does. There's no arguing that. There's also no arguing the way my soul lights up when I'm writing, or reading, or even just talking about the craft with other writers and industry professionals. This level of fulfillment is one I've not had in any of my other careers, and it's one I hold onto when backing the merits of my vision, and the words still to come.

Eventually, I stop work earlier in the afternoon. Take baths with one boy or the other. Play games of Jenga where the toppling of the blocks is the highlight, and no longer a cause for surprise or distress.

*There's so much work*, I used to say. Only it wasn't work, it was time exchanged for cash, which is okay, but it's important to acknowledge the difference between exchanging time for cash and exerting effort to make your wife and kids' lives better.

Because make no mistake, one pays and the other costs, however much it appears to be the other way around. I do my best to be emotionally present for Noah and Josh. Even my parenting-wins, when executed, would likely be something Annaya just does as a matter of course. It would be easy to dispel that as a gender difference; really, though, it's more personal than that. It's about my being able to truly give of myself and still believe there's enough to go around and come back to me when I need that love, and that care.

If I'm being kind, I'm flawed at best. I rarely catch a drink before it spills, we break more plates than at a Greek wedding and I sometimes lose my temper. If I were subject to a performance review, I'd imagine they would say, 'Tries hard but not particularly well suited to the role.'

My imperfections as a parent hit me harder than anything I have previously felt or experienced. They feel like a particularly big deal. I know my inner critic has been humouring me while I've developed my parenting, rather than my writing skills.

Should things start to irreparably affect my writing dreams alongside these visions of being a good dad, then I get the feeling things will go downhill fairly quickly with my inner critic.

Until then, my new workplace is messy, and loud, but you cannot beat the quality of the personnel, or the way they make you feel like you belong there, happy, sad or however else you may feel on any given day.

# Safety and Security

I'm not sure my father-in-law *likes* me.

I get this information from various interactions, including our first meeting, where he grilled me like a detective would interrogate a murder suspect. Now that I'm a dad, I understand this a bit more, yet I will still never know what it is like to first raise a daughter and then find out she's marrying outside of her religion to a *writer* (one of the five swear words of productive society – the others being *poet*, *actor*, *magician* and *street artist*).

Annaya is originally from Mumbai and is of the Parsi faith. I am from Hamilton, New Zealand, and at a push, you could say I was raised as a Jedi.

Our union has always seemed more complicated for Annaya than for me. Her parents want her to be happy, safe and financially secure. My parents also want this for me but mostly leave me to work out the specifics.

It's not hard to see, then, why Annaya's father-in-law, Dinyar, took some time to warm to our union. She had found herself a doctor, only I wasn't that kind of doctor.

The mind of an intensely focused Parsi man whose daughter, once a girl, is now a strong, forthright and independent woman, most likely works something like this:

*I hope she's safe.*

*I hope she's warm.*

*I hope she has friends.*

*I hope her husband remembered to shut the garage door.*

The state of our garage door is incredibly important to my father-in-law. I've received texts and calls about it. On more than one occasion, I have gone outside, only to find my father-in-law pressing the button.

There is something disheartening at that moment, and I always feel more guilty than him for not worshipping the up-down magic of our entry point as much as he does. If I were to reraise my garage door and then close it, he might clasp his hands together with contentment and say, with Yoda-like phrasing, 'Indeed, Laurie. Got it, you have.'

I'm not sure I've ever craved someone's approval more than the approval of my father-in-law. Well, maybe Mike Hussey's if I were playing cricket in the nets, and he showed up specifically to watch me hit a textbook late cut. Other than that, though, my life since meeting Annaya has been a matter of striving and mostly failing to reach Dinyar's belief that I'm not so much an opening batsman as a night watchman, blocking ball after ball in the hope of getting us through to the next day.

Once I was with Annaya, it was like dating and, by extension, trying to impress two people rather than one. When I started looking for jobs after completing my PhD, his nods of approval felt like chocolate to me – I could never get enough. Once, he wanted to talk about taxation, and

I almost asked for a photo of the two of us at the dinner table to document my commitment to keeping better tax records.

The birth of our first son felt like a blessing in more ways than one. My government job felt not so much a nod as a knighthood – a writer who had finally found a better way to make a living and the words to say goodbye to all that. Then, with the birth of our second son, Dinyar seemed to realise that I was not that bad a dad, whatever else my shortcomings.

Once, after the birth of our second son, my father-in-law asked, 'How are you going?'

I said, 'I'm finding it hard.'

I continued, but he said, 'No, not you. I am asking about the boys.'

I laughed and, in time, noted a more significant suggestion that whatever else was going on, being a dad should never be solely about me. I'm not sure I agree with him; while parenting is necessary sacrifice a great deal of the time, for me, that ability to be a kind, present dad starts with knowing what I need and finding ways, when I can, to meet those needs alongside the needs of my boys

When the contract ended on my government job, I lived a worryingly deceitful few weeks where I wore button-up shirts, trousers and dress shoes at every drop-off and pick-up when they were looking after the boys. While their assistance helped my productivity as I set up my own business, it also hurt my self-esteem, igniting doubts that my writing, mentoring and manuscript assessments were not real work but rather a phase to be worked through beyond which lay the next soul-destroying real job.

The pressures on a man to find gainful employment rarely delve further than the idea that they work *somewhere* and get paid to be there. This is the straight and narrow in every sense of the word. There is no room for greater conversations about a man's purpose because our purpose has been predefined. We remain gainful members of society so long as we keep our heads down and, for the most part, do work that most benefits another person, company, or government organisation.

Dinyar and I do not talk all that much. Indeed, my favourite conversations of ours are not actual conversations, but us sitting together in a room with the boys, with the two of them desperate to include one or both of us in a board game, puzzle or game of hand tennis. Though he seemed more at ease with their baby stage, Dinyar still lights up around my boys, and it's clear there are some things on which we will always agree. The first and most crucial point is that these boys are precious, and if we ever feel stressed, exhausted or lonely, we need only look outside ourselves and gaze in awe at these growing, joyful creatures.

When he was younger, my father-in-law raised his siblings practically on his own, working jobs for the pay and not the passion – and as a father, he always put his kids before himself. I must seem quite confronting, even selfish, with my dreams of publication, recognition and readership.

He's wiser than me in many ways. He'll sit with me, as one might sit down a troublesome child, and explain how parenting works – not in the emotional realm, but that of savings, investments and building a nest egg for my boys so that they never have to worry about money.

He also knows his way around property, assets and financial management. I like to hear him talk about it too, all the while pretending I'm well versed in the area and may, once or twice, have discussed such things at a think tank or economic forum.

What would I tell him if I were brave enough?

*I've never known this stuff.*

*I wish I knew this stuff.*

*I see what you are trying to teach me. I want to learn it if you'll teach me.*

*I can now see your guidance is a way to say, 'Take care of yourself, and my child, and her children too. We love you, and we want you to be safe.'*

It is hard to be a new kind of man around Dinyar. More challenging is the knowledge that, unlike him, I must retain one per cent of myself for *me* rather than giving my all to my boys. Such self-care is a necessary alternative to falling back into obsessive thoughts or heightened states that will hinder my ability to be a loving, present parent

Eventually, I tell my father-in-law that I'm building a business out of words – assessment and mentoring and writing when time permits. There's no grand conversation or need to bring me in. Instead, it's his knowledge that I've finally got this. He knows, having seen me with my boys, and spending time looking after them, that I would never start a passion project I could not complete.

'You are excellent parents. I see from the way the boys light up to greet you,' he told me once. 'You're raising great kids.'

I don't tell him how his words buoy our spirits. That Annaya and I spend most nights talking about our boys, gauging approaches, and rethinking strategies. How in awe I am of his daughter – my wife – and the way she takes care of our kids. How she sits with them, actively joining in with their games, how she insists on no books or devices at dinner time to be sure we talk with each other instead.

How she, like her father, has a knack for knowing how to make a child feel loved.

I take photos of my in-laws when they least expect it. Catch their joy at Josh, full giggle, or Noah cuddling up, the way he only does when he knows he can trust the person.

I want to be that kind of son-in-law. Valuing their presence and acknowledging my gratitude. Knowing this will pass and that their words of wisdom, and sheer compassion, will not be around forever.

It's ten o'clock on a Sunday morning when my phone buzzes. It's a text from my father-in-law.

*Your garage door is open.*

I head outside and press the button on the garage wall. Hear the creak of rolling metal.

I walk inside and gaze out of our bedroom window. A

storm's coming. Perth's forever rolling them in and out. Greys gatecrashing spring, bringing rain that swirls from gusty winds.

I pick up my phone and text back, *Thank you*.

# Two Hands

Between Josh's second and third birthdays, I write an email to my mum about my childhood. It's the beginning, or more accurately, the recommencement of a discussion about my upbringing, and the challenges I faced within the family home

Mum takes her time in responding, perhaps because she has the same fears I do as a parent – that at some point, they messed up, even while doing the best they could at that particular time.

Or perhaps that's not what's going on. When I write to her that as parents we are the same, two people with children evaluating our lives at different times in history, she is quick to correct me: we are not the same, because I had four kids and you only have two. We are not the same, she reminds me, because I had to do it on my own and you have a partner to support you. While that stings a little at first, I get her point. My mother was a woman, not a man, living at a different time in history, raising four kids on her own.

We stay mostly stuck in more recent discussions around our familial history. And then one day, Mum gets a call. They've found a lump in her breast. She needs to come up to Perth, so they can investigate further. Mum asks if she can stay. I say, 'Of course,' and so begins a new connection in our relationship.

Mum drives up the next weekend. She calls it her 'cool' car; it's a white hatchback with a stereo that kicks anytime you tweak the volume knob even a little too much too the right, and I guess it is kind of a cool for a woman who's nearly seventy. That night, we sit on the couch in the front half of the house, away from the boys, who are happily sleeping, and closer to Annaya, who has retreated to the bed, her iPad on, and headphones in.

'You doing okay?'

'Yep,' says Mum. 'I mean we don't know that it's anything, not yet.'

We watch some television, and it's Miriam Margolyes, she's travelling around Australia.

'Isn't she wonderful?' says Mum.

'Sure,' I say, thinking of her in *Blackadder.* My mum was an actress too. She was also one of the earliest members of a local theatre group here in Perth, where you get up, tell your story to a moderator and they act it back to you.

'You ever miss acting?'

'I think that boat has sailed,' she says, laughing.

'But do you miss it?'

'Sure,' she says, and stops there.

I stand up, stretch. 'I'm heading to bed.'

'Goodnight, love,' she says, and I lean down into her arms, as she's still on the couch, outstretched. As we hug, I hear the feedback from her hearing aids, a metal scratch that must be louder to her ears to mine.

The next day we arrive at the hospital and head up to the Breast Clinic. Women sit in the waiting room, reading books.

Mum checks in for her appointment. We don't have to wait too long before we're ushered in, and the doctor can bring Mum up to speed.

'So, I imagine you're here for your results.'

Mum nods.

The doctor pauses. 'It's bad news, I'm afraid.'

Mum starts to cry. I put my hand on her arm, while the doctor immediately takes Mum's hand in hers.

'Now, listen, don't you cry, and you're not to worry,' she says. 'We have a high success rate. If we do this.'

'Do what?'

She picks up a pad of paper, upon which shows two women's breasts. She draws a line across the breast, to indicate a mastectomy, which is an operation to remove all breast tissue from a breast as a way to treat or prevent breast cancer, as opposed to a lumpectomy, where they only remove the tumor from the breast.

'It's what we're looking at, our best chance to stop the growth.'

Mum cries some more and then eventually composes herself. 'But it will help?'

The doctor nods. 'We want you to get better. So let's do this, yeah?'

In the weeks and months after, through treatment and recovery, Mum stays when she's up and heads home soon after each appointment.

At first, it's strange to again have her in my home every couple of months. She bonds immediately with the boys, with their hearts not quite as guarded as mine. We start our reconnection by going to the shops (Mum loves to shop,) and watching British comedy. It's something that we've always done: Mum introduced me to *The Two Ronnies*, *The Young Ones* and *The Kenny Everett Video Show*. These days it's panel show purgatory, *Would I Lie to You?* and *8 Out of 10 Cats Does Countdown*. Mum loves Sean Lock, I like Joe Wilkinson, his sense of weirdness.

We don't talk much about the treatment, that's saved for pre-dinner conversation. And we rarely ever use the word 'cancer'.

As the visits continue, I ask her about Dad. About the divorce. About those many things on which I've formed concrete opinions.

It seems I'm wrong about some of those, and in many cases, the greater truth is much more complex and more difficult to process. She tells her truth, never correcting my assumptions, because I'd never bothered to check these with her in the first place. Now it seems such a male thing to do. To take an assumption, carve it into stone. To not know all that much, but to be steadfast in the right to know so little and let it substitute as truth.

I think men do this so as not to appear weak or vulnerable. It doesn't work, though, and instead results in men committed to being right. In my life, I've met men so committed to the pretence of infallibility that they continue to labour a point to their personal detriment. If it achieves anything at all it is really more feelings of isolation in a gender that already knows what it's like to be judged by their ability to hide their feelings rather than expressing them.

My mum is shorter than me. Her hair, once gold, is now platinum grey, while mine is chestnut brown, now growing silver. Sometimes, she still fights with the world, or gets flummoxed with parking, prices or store policy.

She comes up every year for follow-up tests. We watch Miriam Margolyes, Rob Brydon, David Mitchell, or any number of other funny people on the telly that might wrench us from our overthinking minds.

Some memories of my mother are particularly vivid. It's hard to forget her crouched in canola, a huge smile on her face, and how I had to bend down to take the pic. There's a similarly fond memory of the two of us driving, cross-country, The Whitlams up loud, sharing the chorus of 'Buy Now Pay Later (Charlie No. 2)'.

It's more challenging to let go of the times I felt unheard, or the moments I needed more than she was able to give.

For now, there is nothing to address, to argue or revisit. Just the chance that, having cared for her as she looked after me, we might find there's more to us than how things were and the way they've always been.

## Like Riding a Bike

Our son, Noah, is now six years old, and Annaya's keen to switch him from his standard gait to the madcap pedal-frenzy of a pushbike. She's sure that will usher in a new sense of freedom, and the fevered spirit a boy so desperately needs.

Instead, Noah and I wake each Saturday morning to a mutually shared dread on account of her urgings to 'go for a ride'. If we were actually 'going for a ride', that might be enjoyable. Until now, the weather's been miserable, and we've been teaching him at an undercover carpark.

Today we try something a little different and find a spot outside a closed leisure centre on a sunny, warmish day. It's as though we're willing the perfect lesson into being. As if we've now stopped teaching and have begun to pray.

It doesn't go well on those first few runs. My son still can't ride his bike, and I can't bend over all that well to guide him, or I do it, and my back begins to hurt, or I nearly tangle myself up in his back wheel. Just as he says, 'I can't do it!', I again think neither can I, even as Josh rattles past on his three-wheeler.

Noah and I take a break and sit on the kerb.

'You'll get it,' I say.

'Tell me about the time you were learning to ride a bike,' says Noah. 'Tell me about the time you fell off.'

I tell him the whole sad debacle, from the moment I've got it until my hands shake, and the front wheel begins to wobble.

He laughs hysterically, says 'do it again' and so I do it again. It's pretty funny, I'll admit, for there is always something ridiculous about trying to have things in your control, only to stuff it up.

Such things have often caused me great anxiety. These thoughts of a hundred times I slipped up, stuffed up, or said the wrong thing. Even now, as a writer, they continue to create fear, the thought that I might put a word or comma wrong in a sentence. Which would be fine if writing were the creation of a single sentence, but there are hundreds, thousands of sentences in each thing I write.

And yet, in all that counting up of the flaws and failures, I've missed the times it worked, or it was fine, or I wobbled and corrected myself. And, when counting, you very much need to include every item for fair representation.

'Shall we go again?'

He nods, and we lift up his bike: first, a couple of small, tentative steps, and then feet up on the pedals, my hands on his shoulders. And then we start, almost unconsciously, counting together.

'One … two … three … four …'

My hands still held tight, from weeks of 'Don't let go of me'.

'Five … six … seven … eight …'

I let go because he's starting to drift. His feet in motion, his body, looser, and I walk along beside him. Counting to ten, fifteen, and then twenty. Thirty, forty, fifty, and we stop.

'Again?'

He nods, and we turn the bike.

'Annaya!' I yell. 'Let's film this one!'

She raises her phone at arm's length, begins to record, and we look down together, not keen for him to be so acutely aware of being the centre of attention.

'Fifty-one ... fifty-two ... fifty-three ... fifty-four ...'

I keep going because I know every number is another pin on the 'okay' side of the board, and one less on the side of 'not enough'. I'm walking even faster, now up to a jog, as we hit sixty, and then seventy. We're measured now. We hit a speedbump, and the bike slows but doesn't stop.

Eighty, just another number, and I would like to say he's flying along, and that I'm flying alongside him, but in truth, we are going only marginally faster than a dog on its daily walk.

Annaya yells, 'You're doing it, Noah!' and it's like hearing a director's commentary on your life because we are so busy counting, we've forgotten he's riding. The collation of numbers is like the drip, drip from a tap, only infinitely better, and more delightfully predictable than the wobbling of a wheel or rise on the road surface.

By the time we're at ninety, we're past Annaya and Josh, intent on hitting triple figures, and we make it, and he hits the brakes, and we slow to a halt.

'Can I see the video?' Noah says to his mum.

They watch it, two, three times, and then I pick up the bike with one hand and carry it to the boot of the car.

'That was such a good idea with the counting,' says Annaya. 'Where did you come up with that?'

And I could tell her every mistake that's filed away in my mind. And I could mention that these memories are stored not according to a timestamp but according to their emotional intensity. That to remember the good, or even adequate, is harder than to remember the catastrophic. That it is when we count them up that they so clearly outweigh the negative moments when we were small, silly, at fault, or embarrassing.

But I don't tell her this. I say, 'It worked well, didn't it?' counting upward in my mind, another notch on the side of okay.

# Panic

By the middle of 2020, and with the relative glory days of *You Belong Here* now long gone, my inner critic is not so much a kind-hearted coach as a relentless personal trainer, constantly pushing me in terms of what I need to write, and its degree of difficulty.

I actively try to keep such a pointedly critical voice out of how I talk to Noah and Josh. Such negation of it in one area only really means it will in time show up in another area, most often my writing. So, as if on cue, my inner critic's response to my feeling somewhat comfortable in my career appears in fragments, none of which are all that complimentary.

*Keep going.*

*One spelling mistake is a mistake too many.*

*This is not a game. Everyone wants this just as much as you.*

*Win a prize, get your next book published, and then we can celebrate.*

It's exhausting with you. Christ, what do you want?

*You know this is hard, right? I mean far out. I'd have thought you would know by now after seventeen years of doing this that you've chosen the steep, relentless climb.*

What are the other options?

*Write stuff that sells.*

You're fucking with me.

*Yes, I'm fucking with you. I push you because you want to write stuff that matters to you. I keep pushing you because we decided a long time ago that this was your life, and the rules very clearly stated that you'd do it well, or not at all.*

It's funny to spend a life with someone guiding you while rarely questioning the ways in which they seem to guide you.

My inner critic sees each rejection as a warning light on a car dashboard. It thinks that we are not yet at the place where we can rest, despite my successes. In reality, we're in some kind of limbo state, sometimes winning, sometimes losing, never quite there, and yet so much further along than when we started.

I keep going. The funding I've received to write my next book, a collection of short fiction called *Greater City Shadows*, has my inner critic cautious but uncharacteristically supportive. When I secure the editorial services of one of WA's finest writers and editors soon after, it is almost proud of me.

*Now we're talking*, says my inner critic. *You deserve this level of support.*

I'm writing another novel, *The Bear*, at the same time. It's a book about two young men searching for the perfect film location, which leads them to Bulgaria's Rhodope Mountains. While searching, our main protagonist, Brae, meets a bear, is swatted into a tree trunk and falls into a coma. In the second half of the book, the protagonist walks with the bear in his dreamscape. The bear, who's a spiritual being, reflects back Brae's fears, thoughts and inadequacies while leading him back towards his comatose self, in the hope that such awareness has him waking anew, no longer so obsessed with finding perfection.

*So clever*, says my inner critic. *Not only did you get a fellowship to go to Bulgaria back in 2014, but you found a way to incorporate it into your next book. You're always thinking ahead, never letting the present get in the way of your continuing success.*

I wish I could say that my approach to fathering Noah is necessarily more forgiving, but in truth, I struggle to see him drop a ball or spill a drink. That's less about him and, increasingly, more about me. In such moments I consider whether there's a way to mute the inner critic and in the process free up Noah to have a kinder, less conditional relationship with success and achievement.

I continue writing *Greater City Shadows*. I continue assessing other people's work, my inner critic more than willing to scold them for every grammar faux pas or misplaced comma.

My inner critic watches on, mindful that I don't slip up, or get too far ahead of myself. *You should always have a backup when it comes to your writing, it says, because we cannot afford to mess this up.*

Things start to unravel, slowly at first. At an otherwise ordinary meeting with my publisher, I tell her about my funding and how I've been working with an editor. She makes a face, says 'I've been meaning to talk to you. The press is finishing up.'

I sit there, silent. *But I did good*, a voice keeps saying.

'I'm sorry, Laurie,' she says. The rhyme sounds unintentionally comic and gives the opportunity for my inner critic to say, *Geez, you screwed this up.*

I didn't do this.

*Yeah, but you didn't not do it.*

She tells me that with all this in mind, they won't be able to publish *Greater City Shadows* or anything else I write from here on in. They say *You Belong Here* will in time go out of print, and they'll give me copies of my book so I can sell them, like a purveyor of wicker at a craft fair or a fruit seller at the Fremantle Markets.

I work with that, thinking, *You still have* The Bear, and, *There are still other publishers*, and, *Don't you dare fall apart on me now.*

Two Sundays later I take Annaya and the boys down to Hillarys, a beachside precinct that is basically is a car-boot sale version of Brighton in England, or a sun-blasted Coney Island. On the way in there's a newsagent. Papers are a thing we used to read before we had kids, but today we take the punt, *The West Australian* for local news, and *The Australian* for a comically oversized paper from which to try and negotiate the world as it is. I grab *The Australian*'s review section, with Annaya taking the *Weekend Australian* magazine.

It's great to read the books section again, something I did all the time during my PhD, but not so much since Noah, and particularly not since Josh entered our lives. I start with the fiction reviews and recognise certain names from their previous works. Kate Grenville has released a new novel, *A Room Made of Leaves*. I see this as a good sign, as I read her guide, *The Writing Book*, when I first started my career. Soon enough, I move on to non-fiction and then international releases, and it's there, on page six, that I see it.

*The Bear.*

I let out a single, angry laugh. Annaya's busy with the boys so she doesn't notice. I read the review, and it seems the book's central figure and general premise are a lot like mine.

I would like to say that at this point, I shrug my shoulders, mutter, 'Well, shit happens,' but I don't. I tell Annaya, in a tone like someone's stolen my car, or has broken into my house, 'That's my book. He's written my book.'

'Is it the same?'

'Not *exactly* the same, but similar.'

'How could this happen?' she says.

*You took too long to finish it*, says the inner critic. *Hell, you practically gave it to him.*

Noah knocks over his juice, and for a second, I'm distracted, grateful to mop it up. I finish and plop a fistful of orange-tinged napkins, soaked through, on the centre of the table.

'How similar?'

'Similar enough for it to be a problem.'

While Annaya tends to Josh, as he has also splashed juice on his shorts, I ask my inner critic, What do I do? Help me, what do I do?

It says, *I don't know. I'm not sure how you can come back from this.*

I sit there, silent and defeated, until a different quieter voice says, *It's okay. It's not a big deal, we'll just write something else.*

My editor and I meticulously comb the *Greater City Shadows* manuscript in the hope that I might find a suitable publisher. At around the same time, Annaya and I attend a Margaret Atwood interview at the Perth Convention and Exhibition Centre. During the event, she mentions a pandemic on the verge of sweeping the globe. We have no idea what she's talking about. Instead, we just sit there, hoping she'll make another joke soon, as we're not sure we like the fear in her voice, or the insistence on which she continues to state her case.

I submit *Greater City Shadows* to publishers the following week. A couple of weeks after that, the pandemic hits in full force, locking down a number of capital cities in Australia. My grand plan of finding an east coast publisher now seems hopelessly flawed in the new COVID-19 reality.

*This sucks*, says my inner critic. *Keep going.*

What's the point?

*Do you want to be a failure? Is that what you want?*

I never said—

*Well don't be so self-defeated. You know how long it took Manil Suri to get published?*

You told me. I can't remember.

*I can't remember either, but it was a really long time. And did he give up?*

I don't know, I don't even remember the article anymore, it was ages ago.

*Well, maybe think about it each time you feel like cracking the sads.*

For the next six months, I receive kind words regarding the quality of *Greater City Shadows* from people who don't want to publish it. It's like a series of dates where your date leans in to kiss you only to end up sniffing your ear.

The next time I think actively about where I am instead of where I'd rather be, it's at a cafe with my once creative writing PhD colleague and now fellow Doctor of Philosophy, Michelle. She's won runner-up for a national award, a huge deal, so I try to put my failings aside to share the moment with her.

'It's great,' she says. 'I mean, it's exciting, right?'

She apologises for not asking me to write a cover quote for her book. It's this thing she does, assuming that I see each move of hers as a diss on my literary talents. I don't. More often I see each act of hers as a hand upon my shoulder, teaching me how to let things go, and to hold onto what really matters.

I love Michelle in a particularly empowering way. I love that she studied a PhD in creative writing at the same time and the same university as me. I love that she kept in touch afterward, while other equally affiliated people moved states, cut contact or otherwise got on with their lives.

I wonder what her inner critic sounds like. I hope it's not like mine, and that, as she tells me of her success, she swells with pride in all she's achieved.

I mention that the judge of her competition has been caught up in a #MeToo style scandal. I then apologise for having mentioned it. I want to say again, 'This is huge, Michelle, congratulations,' so I repeat myself, and feel a little better.

It's not until we reach the carpark that she asks about *Greater City Shadows*, and I go through the rejections.

'It will get picked up,' she says.

'But what if it doesn't?' I say, and she sees that I'm terrified.

'Oh my gosh, Loz, it's okay.'

But it doesn't feel okay. When I fail, it never feels okay.

•

That night, I take Noah, and Annaya takes Josh into the bedtime routine. Noah's now six years old, so rather than reading him Grug, we throw a bounce-ball up against his bedroom cupboard, with me lying on his bed, and him standing, waiting to catch it. After a while, I slide off the bed, we sit on the floor, facing each other.

'I'm a bit sad,' I say.

'What happened?'

'No one wants to publish my book.'

'What, *Greater City Shadows*?'

I nod.

'Not *You Belong Here*?'

I shake my head. 'That's already published.'

'Oh, that is sad,' he says. 'What will you do?'

'I don't know,' I say. 'I have no idea of what I'm meant to do from here.'

'I'll have a think,' he says, raising his finger to his bottom lip.

'That's really sweet, thanks, buddy.' I stand up, lift him high for a standing cuddle.

He's bigger these days, so it's more of a powerlift than a measured raise, but I hold him close, let his arms cup around my neck, and his feet still dangle a foot or so off the ground, so I swing him back into bed, a kiss on his forehead as he snuggles in, before retreating to the door and turning off the light.

## Cooperation

At about this time I start working with Marie, a creativity coach. Unlike with my psych sessions, a step towards the coaching space feels impressively practical. I tell her what I want to get from our time together. She seems impressed by my drive and dedication. In reality, it's my ego's last stand; I rattle off previous publications, awards, and fellowships to her in the hope they are enough to propel me to my next milestone.

I start by outlining that I'm here to reach more goals. Soon enough, she has me thinking about why I need to reach those goals in the first place.

We meet via Zoom, which is helpful, as it sits her in a space of work, rather than personal development. It also lets me be more honest and less intimidated by what would otherwise be a more intense form of communication and connection.

I sit at my desk with my thighs pushed up against the too short tabletop, and she, I imagine, is in her home office too, a COVID-19 meeting point and post-pandemic reality. At first, we define my inner critic, who has in time become an inner arsehole. Or maybe it once saw the flames on the horizon, yelling, 'Go. We have to go, right now!' and we've been running ever since.

My inner critic says, *Don't listen to her. Or pretend to listen to her but then achieve something really massive, something so amazing that her knowledge, all that wisdom, is rendered redundant and obsolete.*

*Remember Iowa? And how about Bulgaria and the Sozopol Fiction Seminars? Good feelings, huh? And they sure as shit did not come from anyone telling you what to do or from dragging you down into a place of vulnerability.*

*I'll have your back,* it says. *You can stop coaching right now if you want to. No questions asked, I trust your judgement.*

I don't stop because I am utterly, inconsolably miserable. It's a strange thing, too, because successes arrive even as I continue to explore what's really going on inside me. So, when I receive the Henry Handel Richardson Flagship Fellowship for Short Story Writing to travel to Varuna, in New South Wales, I am torn. I've received the green light to again work on *Greater City Shadows*, only now it feels less like a book and more of a burden. I feel as though either the manuscript or me is cursed, and I don't know which one would be worse.

Again, I find the same question. Why can't I just live independently of my inner critic now I have made it to adulthood? When did I get so attached to the inner critic? What's the shame in starting anew and finding new ways to work through life?

The relationship feels constrictive but familiar. Everything it did it seems was out of love. Only I'm no longer sure I want to call it love. It's more just a way to keep me stuck in guilt, shame and fear.

I tell Marie of my recent story acceptances as an alcoholic might tell their sponsor of a relapse. She reminds me these are successes, and worthy of celebration. She points out that it's the inner critic that's even now destroying *these* celebrations, always focused on greater goals rather than celebrating little wins along the way.

'So what exactly is wrong with me?'

She laughs. 'I'm not sure anything is *wrong* with you. Maybe it's time to try some different things.'

'Like what?'

'Well, what would you like to focus on today?'

'I feel like I'm split in two,' I say. 'At war.'

'Okay. Two sides.'

'I think so.'

'And what are those two sides?'

I've never really thought about that, and when I do, the answer's simple.

'They're independence and dependence,' I say, 'and one I really hate.'

She laughs again. 'You hate it or you fear it?'

'Hmm,' I say, and we both laugh. 'So what do we do?'

'Well, and we're getting into the *woo, groovy-groovy* stuff here, but we could do a parts integration.'

'Do we need slides? A projector?'

'No, nothing like that,' she says. 'Close your eyes. Put independence on one hand, and dependence on the other.'

'Gotcha.'

'What does dependence look like?'

‘It’s a giant red iceberg, filled with people, and rough to the touch.’

‘Does it have a sound?’

I pause. ‘Argh.’

‘Are you okay?’ says Marie.

‘No,’ I say. ‘That’s the sound.’

‘And how about independence?’

I smile. ‘It’s a clear iceberg, with me inside. It’s smooth and quiet.’

‘Okay, good. Now, tell me what independence wants you to know.’

‘It says it wants to keep me safe.’

‘And dependence?’

I pause. ‘It’s trying to keep me safe.’

She gets me to view me from further away while my eyes are still closed, this weird director’s commentary thing I’ve done in guided meditations, and I’d like to tell you more, but while I’m under, these things tend to skate by my conscious mind. They’re also easier to process in that space, because in there, I do not have to think so much. In there, I start to wonder if processing and subconscious exploration are actually the opposite of rigid, conscious thought.

We finish up, and I open my eyes.

‘How do you feel?’

‘Good. Not great, I mean let’s not get carried away, but okay. Better. Can we do this again?’ She nods. ‘Thank you,’ I say. ‘I get the feeling I might need to do this a few more times.’

Coming out of the session, it's the first time I've thought of my literary drive as representing independence, finally seeing my current stuck state as a result of putting that independence above all else, and that my focus has pulled so tight over time, forever fixated on ongoing achievement.

All the wins I never fully celebrated. The friends I didn't see for months at a time while working for the next big win, for proof that I would make it.

The feeling that my life and my writing were two very separate things.

I head to the kitchen to make lunch. Annaya is making dahl in a slow cooker. She drains the chickpeas, chops the onions. From the kitchen counter, I spy Josh, who lies not on the couch but on top of the vertical cushions, watching Numberblocks.

'What have you learned buddy?'

'What's five plus four plus three plus two plus one?'

'Fifteen.'

'What's four plus three plus two plus one?'

'Ten.'

'Daddy, what's—'

'Six,' I say thankful for his predictable pattern, and grateful that, at this particular time, I can give the right answer.

# HOLDING ON

# Sanctuary

Being a writer can be a gateway to next-level existential panic, even while you are doing the job you love best in all the world. It is a constant reminder of the precarious nature of one's life and career, and the begrudging admission that, of all the things in the world, the only one a writer can control is the words upon the page.

However, solace abounds for the creative professional if they are willing to track greater connections outside of their own sometimes myopic thoughts, and perhaps that's the most valuable gift: experiencing our thoughts not in a vacuum but as part of a greater conversation. In this respect, even this text, as it's being written, is an interpretation of things I've seen and read, and a collaboration with broader discussions about anxiety and its relationship with kindness, compassion, authenticity and vulnerability.

Beyond fiction, some of those texts more influential to me are, unsurprisingly, from the fields of parenting and gender studies. Steve Biddulph's *Manhood* entered my life during my adolescence, at a point when I could easily have turned tough rather than gentle. More recently, Maggie Dent's *Real Kids in an Unreal World* gave me an accessible blueprint from which to create the building blocks to my kids' resilience and self-esteem, and Rick Morton's *My Year of Living Vulnerably* had me wanting to continue a much greater conversation around men, intimacy, and necessary tenderness.

My calmer, more patient thoughts often echo those heard while listening to Jack Kornfield's Dharma talks on loving kindness. Brené Brown's *The Gifts of Imperfection* profoundly shifted my willingness to be vulnerable and authentic both on and off the page: Johann Hari's *Lost Connections* reaffirmed my own deep need for meaningful friendships as part of managing my anxiety, and Kristin Neff opened me up to the study of self-compassion in her book of the same name, in the process allowing me to feel necessary grief and disappointment in those moments when I came up short in my chosen career.

One of the better parts of being a writer, however, is to cast the net even wider. Indeed, if you asked me to name another artist who inspired me at a pivotal time in my life, then it's Glaswegian industrial-rock artist Rico, and his album *Sanctuary Medicines.*

I first heard Rico while travelling around England and Scotland, aged twenty-two. Britpop was huge at the time – and, with some notable exceptions, the bigger bands were mostly a collection of twats, tossers and wallies, known for being 'lads', acting out and avoiding any attempts to be insightful or genuine.

Rico was not at all like them. But we'll get into that, soon enough.

I worked at Yates's Wine Lodge, down a back street in Aberdeen most nights. We earned one pound, eighty pence an hour, with the expectation we'd make up the amount necessary to live on through tips. Morven made crazy tips, Aoife amassed glass after glass spilling over with pound notes. If I was lucky, I would get one pound fifty extra in tips, and could afford a bouquet of 'cheese and chips' from the all-night joint down by the docks.

Each night, we'd get the same sonic assault: 'Livin' La Vida Loca', 'Mambo No. 5' and 'Miami'. All the while, I'd serve vodka and Irn Bru, pints of 'heavy' (beer) and Bacardi Breezers to the youth of Aberdeen. Results would vary; some would get off their faces, some would get busy on the dance floor, and some would get off with each other on that same sticky dance floor, or outside, under the shade of a shop awning.

I'd wake up sick from the relentless shitness of it all, nursing a headache and cursing my life. Most days, I'd eat a late breakfast or early lunch, have a shower, and then walk the streets of Aberdeen to keep warm until it was time to head back to work. I couldn't stomach the thought of returning most days, such was the cumulative effect of that kind of atmosphere that would make you move planets just to get away from it. And so, on a whim one afternoon, I went somewhere else before the start of my shift.

On Union Street, the sun had already started to set. I passed Frankenstein Pub, a ropey horror-themed bar, that admittedly served better beers than most in the area, before crossing the road and walking on to Virgin Megastore.

I headed straight to the listening stations, slid on the headphones and CD number one stared back at me, and I mean literally. An eye took up the entirety of the CD cover, with the words, *Rico <Sanctuary Medicines>* emblazoned on it.

I liked listening to new music – I worked in radio in the lead-up to my trip to the UK – and so pressed play. A guitar riff hit, lone, repeating in isolation, before Rico came in, throaty and already a bit pissed off. From there, it was on for the next five minutes, a sonic barrage of self, and a declaration of intent like few I'd heard before, or since.

Lyrics like doctrines, thoughts as sharp as razors, played on throughout the album. It was a necessarily pissed-off, unapologetic ride where the only rule was to cut the shit and admit how you're really feeling.

I quit my job at the wine bar that night, got a job at a cinema instead, and sought films, songs and people that were similarly raw, real and vulnerable.

Things would have stayed beautifully self-contained on that trip to the United Kingdom, with Rico a brief but welcome interlude in my lost winter, until I find myself again stuck in an identity crisis, writing stories with no one to publish them.

With my heart rate impressively high, I head to the website for Behind The Noise, the Education Program he set up with a friend in 2011 to help passionate, dedicated younger musicians learn more about the industry. I'm not so young these days, nor am I musician, although I've always loved his music. So, I begin an email to him, and write out my hopes and fears seeking greater connection and the continued pursuit of my artistic dreams.

In reaching out to a relative stranger, I'm mortified that

I have somehow circumvented common sense and veered into vulnerability. Still, I've never got all that far by pretending I could do things on my own and have achieved sweet fuck-all by sitting in my loneliness and assuming no one could ever understand the depths of my emotional pain.

Rico's response, when it arrives the next day, is considered and generous. Like me, he is working on a new project, and like me, he is not yet sure how it will turn out. It's an exciting part of the process, wherein the artist is both in and outside of their art and so my fears about outcomes are revisited in his world as opportunities to grow, and learn, and try new things. In a follow-up email, I tell him about my challenges with my second book, *Greater City Shadows*. Again, I'm honest, and vulnerable, and I tell him I'm scared that it will never get published.

What makes me think it's safe to do this? Well, in Rico's music, I have always felt an authenticity of purpose, and a willingness to sit with deep emotional conflict. While a psych might have a better hot take for what's affecting me and how at this point in my life, I would hazard a guess that Rico knows more about what it means to be a flawed, fragile, and understandably frustrated human being and to live in the artistic rather than the analytic space.

Rico released his second album independently after issues with his label, and I assume he'll tell me to do the same. Instead, he is honest, and while not confrontational, he's at the very least, necessarily challenging:

*Sometimes as an artist, it can be difficult to take criticism but at times this might be exactly what you need, finding the line where you take or refuse the advice is the really tricky bit. Alternatively, if you have 100% belief in what you do then listen to no one and push through, but be careful, this belief isn't a shield for you to hide behind.*

He finishes his email with the words *Not sure if any of this helps*. But it all helps. Him taking the time to read my words. Getting back to me with a genuine, thoughtful response. His willingness to see a stranger – albeit one well versed in the life, times and tracks of Ricardo Capuano – as a friend he's not yet met. Later, I find out that was just the type of person he was: a kind, generous guy willing to share advice, insight, or companionship.

In my reply, I thank him for his time and, although I don't mention it, I'm also grateful for his candour and his responding without any sense of judgment. I don't know what that means to him; for me, that generosity of spirit, and that sharing of wisdom, compassion and insight is the closest thing I've found to faith and a shared humanity.

Closer to home, I catch up with my friend and fellow writer, Ethan. When I started writing, he seemed to be living the life I one day hoped to live as a published novelist. Two years after I began writing, my then girlfriend gave me a copy of Ethan's award-winning novel with an inscription that said, 'One day, this will be yours.'

From that point on, his book felt a light guiding me towards what was possible for my own writing. In interviews, the clarity of his thoughts, and his willingness to do what needed to be done for the sake of the work felt deeply reassuring to me; a statement of intent not dissimilar to my own, and a reminder that I wasn't alone in pursuing a life forged in the creation of literature.

Ethan and I did not meet until I'd nearly finished my PhD, and he was beginning his. In the time between reading his debut novel and us meeting again at university, our paths now seemed closer than was previously the case. While I had only recently published my debut novel, and he'd published his much earlier, we'd both struggled with the ups and downs of the writer's life and with juggling our careers and parental responsibilities.

He has two kids, like me, and struggles, just like me, and yet it's also not lost on me that while Ethan continues to write, his wife, also a creative, has found it more difficult to continue her practice. Rachel Power called this 'The Divided Heart' in her book of the same name. Seeing it manifest in a couple I'm good friends with really brings that reality home, however, and I'm sure it's a subject most dads might otherwise barely register; that on some level, it's much harder for a mother to continue to 'do the work' than for a father in that same position.

Ethan and I talk a lot about the craft, and he shares with me fragments, good and challenging, of his journey as a writer. To me, these are everything in terms of creative insight, for if there's one thing none of the older Western Australian male writers prepared me for, it's hardship in one's career, as opposed to one's life.

It's understandable that these men might want to avoid their most vulnerable moments as writers. However, it's also unhelpful for those writers who have come since. With so few men being willing to state such setbacks on the record – and much respect here to WA author Craig Silvey who recently brought up such a setback in his own career – any male writer, and indeed any man who is willing to be that vulnerable deserves not only my respect, but the thanks and respect of anyone who has felt the effects of men not so willing to get in touch with their greater emotional complexity.

As for Ethan, he has a bite for his latest book, a biography. What to say to a writer who has patiently waited fifteen years for his next opportunity despite already being a considered, well researched and passionate author? How to let him know that while my road to a debut full-length publication was long, it was all the more manageable knowing the two of us could wait there together, sharing thoughts, philosophy, and reading recommendations?

In the end, I just say congratulations, as his is a return that's well deserved, and many years in the making.

# Faltering

Things first get much easier, and then much harder in relation to parenting in a COVID-19 reality.

Between two and three years of age, Josh seems to regress. He develops a high-pitched squeak that really throws me off my writing game. In the past, when something similar occurred with Noah, I'd go our local café and while away an hour or two. Only now, they're all shut, and no one seems to know what's going to happen from here, not just in Perth, but in the world as a whole.

At this point, I would typically go our local cafe and while away an hour or two, only they're all currently shut, and no one seems to know what's going to happen from here, not just in Perth, but in the world as a whole.

The noise levels at home are particularly catastrophic, not helped by Annaya's contested but necessary recent decisions to pull up the carpet, put in floorboards, take out the noise-dampening curtains and replace them with venetian blinds.

'We took out the carpet because of Noah's asthma,' she reminds me.

'What about the curtains?'

'The curtains were *ugly*,' she says, and flicks the kettle on.

I tell Annaya that the noise levels in the house are now catastrophically loud. She looks at me as if I am insane.

'If they're too loud, then wear headphones.'

That's the kind of phase we are in as a family, where it's more practical to wear headphones than it is to ask for a minute or two's peace.

We get through as best we can until eventually things catch up with both of us. Annaya is sunk by the endless washing of clothes and the organising of four different meals (don't ask) for the family. I'm near nervous exhaustion from the screams, squeaks, and bins overflowing. We think we can somehow keep it together, but unfortunately, we can't, and it's then that we slip up with our youngest, and at this time, most labile child.

It's a Saturday afternoon at around two thirty, and we're driving back from Ethan's fortieth birthday party. The party was eighties themed. On that note, much respect to Ethan who comes as Robert Smith from The Cure, the Mount Everest of dress-up characters. While my boys are suitably attired in fluoro green and pink head and wristbands, I have not followed suit, as I quite famously can't do costumes since attending what I thought was a ninth birthday dress-up party as Dracula, with white face make-up and a blood trickle from my lips. Except that when we got there, it wasn't a dress-up party.

Looking across the room at Ethan's party, I saw a similarly plain-clothed Michelle, and so we bonded, talking writing, and clinking together our pint-sized glasses of lemon, lime and bitters in celebration of Ethan's big day.

Ethan spoke about the importance of other authors in his life and mentioned Mish and me in his speech. The more significant implication was that as writers, we survived primarily thanks to the kindness, good grace and companionship of those like us, similarly committed to a life in writing. In my life, an email from Ethan or a text from Michelle had often arrived when I might otherwise have felt profoundly alone in my writing pursuits. So, while the feeling was mutual, I'm not sure I could ever have put things as articulately as he did.

We'd done well that day, one of the rare occasions when all four of the family attended a social gathering. The party was held upstairs at a pub – nearly the highest degree of difficulty for a family outing outside of a trip to the city centre – but we'd split up when needed, coming together, if only briefly at various points.

Going home, we were happy, if a little tired. Noah wanted a berry smoothie – he always does – and so, having pulled into the garage, first Noah got out of the car, blocking my exit, as it's a tight garage. I followed him, opened the front door, and headed into the kitchen.

We walked in, and I pulled out a Noah-sized bag of berries, one kilo of frozen fruit from the freezer. I took out the blender, filled the jug with some water to free up the fruit once the blades started moving. Annaya walked in, unpacked the bags, danced around me and Noah. She took some dishes, put them in the dishwasher. Grabbed a cracker and ate that too.

And then she looked at me, eyes wide.'Where's Josh?'

'What do you mean?'

'I mean, "Where's Josh?",' she said. 'Didn't you get him out of the car?'

'I thought *you* got him out of the car.'

'Oh, shit.'

We race out, and Josh is bawling in a way I've not previously heard. They're long, protracted wails. She holds him and he's fighting it. I go to hug him too, but he turns his head away.

She sits on the front bench outside, facing him. He won't face her, though, and continues to cry. Part of me wants her to take him inside as quickly as possible, to cover up our obvious mistake. Another part of me just wishes we could go back to ten minutes earlier and do it right this time.

We get through that day, apologising over and over to Josh, and inside we're still upset with ourselves. On some level, we know it's not a life-changing mistake; we still feel it so keenly, that failure and the effect it had on our boy.

A friend laughs and says this is just the first of many times we'll do this while realising the impact it has had upon our child. That's not to mention the times we've *already* done something and not realised.

Josh brings it up many times in the weeks that follow. That is problematic given he's about to start day care, for one day a week. When we take him to the shops, or to a movie, or to iPlay, he asks can we please not leave him in the car again.

Parenting can be brutal. You try to set up a safe, supportive space, but you're only two people, with needs, jobs, and demands on your time, just like anyone else. Often you slip up, and often you need help outside of the family unit. At some point, unless you're very lucky, you may have to enlist the people who work in childcare, hoping they know how much trust it has taken you to even consider the option.

Each one of those early drop-offs feels like a betrayal. Leaving Josh in a room with no familiar faces. A changing cast of staff from day to day. A handful of hours, if only for Annaya and I to work.

Soon enough, there's a spike of confirmed COVID-19 cases in Western Australia, increasing the risks of sending Josh to day care. Then Annaya's parents offered to take him instead for those same reasons. I took them up on this offer as a circuit-breaker, not yet ready to leave him in the lurch but needing to catch up with work. Or, if my work could in any way be delayed, I would see him crying, note the sniffle, say, 'He's not full-strength,' and keep him home with me, rather than sending him to day care.

My work begins to suffer. My mental health also suffers as I adjust to working from home. It's tough to fit a full-time business into twenty hours a week, not to mention the bleed of childlike cries and calls and bouncing balls, or the cacophonous bang on the door once they've returned from school.

In time, we again consider day care. And in time, Josh again struggles with the idea. Mornings of dread, of holding him tight, as if to make up for the absence. Cries of 'I don't want to go to day care!' on the days preceding.

Annaya and I, always wondering if we're doing it right. Hoping that, if we are not, then that at least they'll feel only a moment of distress rather than the anchored feeling of being alone, or abandoned.

The first two weeks are a nightmare. In week three, it seems he's better adapting to the routine. The next two weeks, we encounter one of the biggest problems in booking your child into day care for a Monday – the expanse of public holidays – and so, with another week off, he regresses into not wanting to go the very next week.

As a practising psychologist, Annaya mentions the importance of the circle of security. She says in some ways that's why day care matters; it sets the child up for the belief that their parent can leave and come back in a predictable pattern.

'How can you tell if it's working?'

'You can't. You do the best you can, and hope that it's enough.'

I'm not sure when things shift. It seems, one day, not much later, that he is finally ready to go to day care. That, rather than seeing a room full of strangers, he has found a place to go 'play'. It's almost a workplace of his own, from which to return and recount stories from the day.

I breathe a sigh of relief. I thank the stars. I pray that one day he will only barely remember that time we came home and went inside without him.

I ring Mum to talk it through. She reminds me of the time we left my sister, Eve, at the fun park, and had to drive back to get her.

'Her face,' I say.

'She was *furious*,' says Mum, laughing. 'As a parent, you will mess up, that's inevitable.'

I tell her about the guilt at the day care drop-off. She says Luke used to cling to the door frame when she tried to get him into the room. A necessary rite of passage, perhaps. A casualty of the modern working world, and the very definition of a can't-win situation.

Just as things appear to be going well, they flare up again with Noah, this time after he closes the cupboard door on me as I'm walking out, and cracks me hard on the head.

'Mate, what are you doing?'

'Sorry,' he says.

'Not *sorry*,' I say. 'It's not okay.'

'I thought—'

'Well don't think, use some common sense!' Only the 'sense' comes out too firm. Noah's face changes, and, *No, no, no, please don't cry*, and it's too late, the tears start coming down his cheeks, and I hold him close, saying, 'Mate, hey mate, it's alright, Daddy's sorry.' At that point I stop talking but I can't stop thinking about the moment his face changed. In that moment, I'm that angry dad, the one I never understood when I was a kid.

It is not the only time I snap at Noah. Over time, these things pop up, moments where it's not that you're clinically anxious, or depressed, it's just all too much. Being an uninvolved parent is a walk in the park, but if you're taking things seriously, and tracking the potential impact of your parenting on your child, then your head begins to spin from even a cursory glance at parental legacy.

My father tells a story about receiving a call from the corner shop to tell him Trent, then five years old, was stealing lollies. I'm horrified by each detail: from my brother, then tiny, having travelled half a kilometre to get to the shop, to the 'what are the chances?' feel of it all. Hearing stories like that, I like to think we're more attentive parents than the previous generation. It rarely feels that way, however, and I sometimes wonder if it was better to have not had a world of parenting advice at your disposal as you fumble, trip or occasionally misstep.

When Annaya and I are in sync as parents, we are *on*, catching dropped toys before they hit the ground, and reaching for the arms of either of our boys when they're about to throw a punch. We slap on bandaids as though they were already unwrapped; we butter toast and plate-up jaffles with pit-stop precision; we make up far-fetched tales that have our boys giggling; as the stories progress, we leave them nestled on our cradling arm, half asleep even as we utter our end paragraphs, and then gently lift them off our biceps, tiptoe out, and hug each other in the kitchen, a job well done.

Outside that, though, the stress continues to build. Depending on the day, Annaya and I can be like dormant volcanoes, calm for the most part, only then we suddenly erupt. While the impetus is usually fairly catastrophic – an overflowing bath with water gushing out onto the tiles, that kind of thing – our reactions are still ugly and surprising, even to us. I mean, it's not like we're still new to parenting at this stage.

Should we forgive ourselves? Of course. Do our reactions

greatly impact on the child? Well, I guess it depends on the child and on the circumstances. Still, most likely, yes, they very much do, so while there's room for some forgiveness and self-compassion, it's that desire to be a good parent that ensures a moment's blow-up doesn't in time become the norm.

A friend says that we're barely getting started. She tells me there will be times later on when it will be increasingly difficult to like them. When they're smelly, or sweary little things. 'When that happens,' she says, 'You look them in the eye, say, "I see that you're upset, and I'm sorry if that's my fault, but remember, I always love you, okay?"' And that there will also be times when they don't much like us, not because we have changed, but because they are changing.

I can't imagine such times. I want to keep Josh this small forever. To hold him close, like he's a baby joey. To protect him, to play with him, and keep him giggling, wondrous, and forever curious, all at once.

And yet, within that wonder, there's also this guilt, and this persistent feeling I am failing my child, despite wanting so much just to love, nurture or protect them.

Annaya talks about it often. She says, 'What are we going to do, Laurie?' about all kinds of things, from Noah's new class list to swimming lessons, to the more recent observation that now we have two children, neither is getting much quality time with either of us.

I sometimes think these moments are reminders; a chance

to step back from the madness; to see that we need self-care as much as they do. It's not always clear how we get that, however, and so more often than not, you have two tired parents on the precipice, and you can only hope the mistakes you make are quickly rectifiable.

That's where things can get unimaginably tough. I know from my own childhood how much things can escalate on the back of a bad break-up, and how quickly one or both parents can lose sight of the bigger picture when they're focused on their own understandable, and at times, unbearable pain.

As parents in this age, we still don't know what effect our phone usage, and constant gazing at screens, will have on those children born into the age of mobile technology. It may be the next mental health epidemic in the making, or it may be part of our own ability to switch roles, tasks and requirements, staying busy so as not to feel too overwhelmed throughout a day of peak moments.

Any progression towards accepting our imperfections is bound to hit snags. Ironically, it's our desire to be great parents that usually causes them. It's easy to knock it out of the park with one kid but throw two, three or four into the mix, and the standards will inevitably start to slip.

The hope is that in time, both we and our kids might see stuff-ups alongside triumphs. I think many fathers of my generation would sooner not revisit those moments where they fell short. We figure that by doing this, we'll not have it recalled, over and over, by somebody else – exhibit 'A' as to why we are fundamentally fucked.

Kids aren't like that, though. More often than not, they're just trying to understand; to make maps around thoughts and emotions, so that neither are confusing.

Another day brings another mess-up. I come home and Noah's cars are everywhere. Straight away I'm into him: 'Come on man, clean this up, it's not cool, Noah, not cool at all.' Not even a 'hello' or 'I love you, bud', and I'm too busy telling him off I don't bother to hear what he's trying to say to me.

I knock on Noah's door a couple of minutes later, and he's sitting on his bed.

'Can I come in?' A small nod.

I say, 'Hey mate, I'm sorry about before. It wasn't okay, and I shouldn't have said it.'

'Why did you say it?'

'I don't know. I was tired.'

'You rest, Dad, it's okay,' says Noah.

'I'm all right. I'm sorry, really. I'm doing my best, you know, just sometimes I mess things up.'

He nods. 'You were too firm. Before, you were too firm.'

'I know, I'm sorry.' We cuddle. 'Thanks, buddy.'

'Okay,' he says, and for tonight, maybe that's enough. Maybe, as parents, we get another chance to do better so long as we remain accountable, and are willing to be flawed, and seen as such, while doing an underappreciated, at times unimaginable and difficult job.

## Suburban Kings

When we returned to Perth from Melbourne, I was dreading living too far out from the city centre. In the end, we do live relatively far out, though it's not a bad place to raise our kids. It is not a blue-chip suburb as such, more a come-as-you-are kind of joint. 'G'day', or at the very least, a nod of your head, is mandatory on your morning walk, and there aren't many locals you won't eventually bump into if you spend enough time at the local IGA.

What do I find toughest out here? Really, the potential for time alone to grow into feelings of isolation; the majority of my time when I'm not alone in a home that's loud, chaotic, and often feels indifferent to my need for peace while working through a draft, edit, or manuscript assessment.

Thankfully, my neighbour Brent is in a similar situation, and much better at reaching out than I am. He's the father of two boys like me. He's a top bloke, too: beanpole tall, less mullet and more buzz-cut, with a smile almost perpetually on his dial.

Brent is also a dynamo at any number of manual tasks, and I am impressively crap at all kinds of handiwork. It's not only that I'm bad at it; many times, I make things worse. Give me a water filter to install and I'll ensure there's running water … all over the cupboards, dripping down onto the floor, a sudden torrent stopped only when I go, *Oh shit*, and I finally find the one right tap with which to stem the flow.

When I lost the key to our side-gate padlock, I called Brent over with his boltcutters. When I needed to put on a new trampoline mat, he came around, did one thing that made the whole thing work, and then left, like a DIY Superman. You think I'm joking; he even has a costume of sorts, almost always dressed in yellow ochre, an Australian amber, if you will, as if to say, 'For God's sake, be careful, Laurie. Order is restored, and the world is again safe for dads born without a practical bone in their body.'

Mostly, when living out here, I've been scared I wouldn't fit in. Often, I don't, mostly because of my studies – I mean, it's not all that common to find film majors and PhD graduates in creative writing this far north of the main universities. Still, that's okay, because there are a few authors scattered in and around my region. I walk with two such blokes once every couple of weeks and have had a fair few coffees with debut authors and emerging writers similarly looking to turn a hobby into their passion. So, while I didn't fit in where I thought I would, as I'm likely one of very few dads with the gall to prioritise passion above all else in my career, there are more than enough people in the greater community who want to share an afternoon, or talk about the craft, so as not to leave me totally lonely.

In terms of likeminded males, there are really just the three of us out here in me, Brent and Nick. We're not so much strange as sensible. We're most attuned to simple joys that always involve and mostly revolve around our kids, like playing games (board, video and sport-related) with them and passing on fragments of knowledge we've found interesting or insightful. We play cricket with our kids in hallways, and frisbee out back. We love takeaway nights, and long, sprawling conversations about what we got ourselves into by becoming dads.

So we talk, and talk some more, in the hope of finding workable ways to parent in this volatile, often unpredictable society. Our consensus on what it means to be a present dad, rather than one who happens to live with his kids, is as follows:

- It's hard.
- It's tiring.
- It's a noisy business, that's for sure, and they fight over anything, and my God, the noise when they start fighting.

After that, we usually share an issue we had with our specific kids, opening up to vulnerability before carefully steering things back to some semblance of competence. These endings usually look something like this:

- We got them an ice-cream.
- We had an ice-cream.
- We gave them a cuddle.

- We watched *Inside Out* to help both them and us learn more about our feelings.
- We did all of the above, and man, *Inside Out* is such a good movie. Not perfect, of course, but it's great to tell our kids it's okay to feel whatever they need to feel; that they're not a pain, and never a burden.

Being a dad is undoubtedly easier than being a mum. That's mainly because most fathers don't worry as acutely about their children as do mums, and they also, though not always, parent without being aware of all the mother does behind the scenes. If they do find out, the minutiae are mind-boggling, with the organisation of appointments, the informal networking with other mums, and the complex arrangement of play dates all somehow sorted, week-in and week-out.

The downside of all that is that dads are often nowhere near as connected to the other dads in their child's class as mums are to one another. Even if we *do* know these dads, or have met them at parties, there is still the tyranny of two hundred years of blokedom to work through. That history of talking guff rather than feelings means you'll talk a lot about the footy or the weather before either of you dip even a toe into your emotional journey as fathers, or the most challenging thing you're currently facing at home in relation to your kids.

Also, being a dad can feel at times a different kind of lonely to being a mum, as for so long we've treated our feelings as enemies rather than comrades. I mean, that's the big dance, right? Emotional literacy. A place where you belong. Where everybody knows your name, and they're always glad you came. Only it's not a pub for me these days. While I'm still partial to a bit of Chisel, I have moved past rowdy renditions of 'Khe Sanh' and declarations of love after one too many beers. I'm no longer willing to make the already hard task of parenting more challenging by getting into a punch-up, snogging a stranger, or trying to break David Boon's tinny drinking record.

All of which goes some way to explain why, when Brent rings to invite me and my boys to frisbee golf on a sunny Saturday morning, I say, 'Let's do it!'

The day itself is summer-still, classic Perth, thirty-two degrees, and only getting hotter. The frisbee golf course is nearby, as it turns out – my apologies to Woodvale, which is clearly more up on extreme sports than I ever expected – and frisbee golf is golf, but with frisbees. I'm not sure how frisbees met golf. Hell, I didn't know they even lived in the same suburb. My only rationale for the shift from ball to disc is that golf has always been a little bit dangerous, what with the rock-hard golf balls being hit at high speeds, and the fact that you're literally carrying lightning rods with you as you make your way around the course.

For now, I'm up for this new hybrid sport. At least I won't get hurt, I think, as I pack, well, nothing, and then head to the oval, finding Brent already there, his kids dancing around him.

Hole one is a belter of a green; I'm kidding, it's like all the other holes, only it's the first hole, so it's pretty much a straight line. Do I get a hole in one? Well no, I get a hole in seven.

On hole two, Noah does a ripper of a throw. On hole three, Brent's eldest son, Alby, side-slings a beauty, and it lands right near something that looks like a Doctor Who prop but is apparently the hole. On holes one to five, Brent does a series of throws, with each more impressive than the last. I swear he is this close to doing a Jordan shrug but instead he says, 'Good effort,' each time I throw a frisbee into a tree. I'm coming fourth by the end of five holes. I'm whipping Josh's butt, but that doesn't really count because he is two years old, and not playing.

On hole six, it's Ben's turn to go first. He's Alby's brother, and a couple of years younger than Alby and Noah. I shift to the side of the tee-off and take a couple of steps back so as not to be in his flight path. Ben pauses, as if to check the wind. Then steadies, bends down, and give that frisbee his most herculean throw.

I can't tell you much about what happens after that. I see a frisbee veer in my direction but my brain flashes up a huge 'no-sale' sign, unable to comprehend what's hurtling towards me. From there, I fall to my knees. I raise my hand to my left eyebrow to soak up the sweat. Only once I pull my fingers down, there's no sweat, only blood.

'Are you okay?' says Brent.

'No,' I say, as blood starts dripping on the grass. 'A bit of a mishap.'

'You want us to play through?'

'I'm going home,' I say, waving most likely at a bank of trees rather than at Brent, as I lift my t-shirt to the wound to stem the bleeding. 'Can you take the kids?'

'We'll play through,' says Brent. 'Let us know if you're okay, okay?'

It's the first time I've left my boys with another parent. But then, Brent is no ordinary dad, despite his son being neither the best nor most accurate frisbee thrower of the family.

I go home, put on first one bandage, and then another, until eventually, Annaya convinces me to see the doctor. I get there and the doctor stiches the wound, although my headache's worse than any of that.

'Can you text Brent?' I message Annaya. 'See that the boys are okay?'

Annaya texts back, moments later. 'They're having a great time,' she says. 'Lucky for frisbee golf, hey?'

Later, an hour or so after the drop-off, Brent shows up with both the boys and a box of Ferrero Rocher to say sorry. A couple of weeks after that, we're back with the boys, this time to play minigolf, and this time I stand well back and let their golf clubs swing like striking cobras.

Brent's also good at minigolf, although this time we don't keep score. We hang out with our kids, laugh often, and hit the occasional metaphorical bunker on our way to being the best dads we can possibly be.

# We Belong Here

In the second half of 2020, there's very little time to do anything other than parent. Once the kids are down, and in the middle of new modes of operation during frequently changing COVID protocols, we find moments where we might otherwise catch up on things, but it's at that point when we need winding down the most.

Annaya binge-watches television while swiping on her phone. I ride an indoor bike, looking like a Cadel Evans who has let himself go. I'm searching for ways to remove my belly, which first showed up when we had a baby boy and expanded when I changed my soups for late night snacks and sweet treats.

I am no longer on my anti-anxiety medication – seven years have somehow passed so quickly, while the days at times seemed endless – and I now process things more actively. Going inwards, rather than out.

My loneliness has rarely abated throughout my life. It is now more manageable and more of a clue on what I might need at any given time: try feeling lonely as a child tickles you or you're playing four-square with your eldest son. And yet there are still echoes from the past, an ache that remains, and may do so for the rest of my life.

My father was also often lonely. An on-call doctor, he would often be summoned to the hospital at ungodly hours. I felt a pang of sadness whenever I heard the car start in the early hours of the morning; I imagine he was similarly sad at having to leave us.

When sitting with my father, he often tells me stories of his younger days; he and his brother armed with pellet guns, shooting at each other up and down the stairwells at their expansive Plymouth home; a night, rolling his father's MG out of the family home, and down the driveway at age fourteen; and, later, raids of the unlocked medicine cabinet in search of the right party starter at college. These memories seem so different from the dad I witnessed growing up. Perhaps that's the real gift of children. You lose your partner and your youthful exuberance but gain these tiny, trusting things who need you to honour their trust in you as a father and role model. You lose some mates and gain a great deal of purpose.

I sit in our now quiet living room, thinking back to us as a couple, before the kids came along. First date coffee catch-ups that ended only when the place needed to shut; a home in Camberwell, long before nappy changes and early morning wake-ups; weekend mornings in half-slumber, cuddles and kisses, a to-do list of two until reluctantly we'd get up, make coffees and teas, and then cuddle on the couch.

All things change, of course, and Noah and Josh are now the stars in my sky. This doesn't make me miss Annaya any less, though, nor does it help with ways in which to embrace my new reality.

How to ease that loneliness? By reaching out. Only for one reason or another, both my father and I have struggled to do this sometimes. To do it requires trust. We both want to trust. In the case of my father, you don't get married three times without believing in things like love and trust. And yet, when we trust in love, we risk losing those other things we need; acceptance, belonging and friendship.

That's why I was more than happy for him to move in with me when he split with his second wife, and likely why he welcomed me back into the state, and his home, when I broke up with the girl I followed to Queensland. It's easy to feel lonely when your present abruptly becomes your past. What else to do at that point but find a familiar, supportive space in which to heal?

To be alone is of course not the same as being lonely. Now that I am a father, I often very much enjoy times of solitude. As a writer, time in reflection feels the opposite of lonely. In this respect, my writing too helps me meaningfully – as opposed to dutifully – reach out to others, with the hope that it makes me and my reader feel less alone.

At other times, I need to talk to a friend. It's a profound way to compare realities; to anchor motivations and life goals; to talk honestly and openly in a discussion that in no way touches on farts, bums, or Mario Kart.

I regularly keep up with Will and Rae, two friends from school. We're a surrogate family of sorts. Rae's the caring mum, bringing homemade muffins and enveloping us in soothing, soulful hugs. Will's the quiet but thoughtful dad, the quintessential top bloke, who listens when you talk and carefully considers each response. And me? I guess I'm the kid, forever wide-eyed, needing to bring us together for the good it does us, always there to remind them that they're loved and appreciated, however long has passed since the last time we caught up.

We mark births, deaths and marriages within the class of 1994. We do picnics in the park or dinners at my place. Because while many have gone, we are still here, bruised but grateful, leaning into trust, love and loyalty.

I have another mate, Jack, from my undergraduate studies at uni. So much has changed in both our lives since we first made short films in ECU's concrete block of a university, and yet, when we catch up, it's as if we're back in first year. Making jokes to the point that no one else gets a look-in during the conversation. No heavier things to unpack, or woes to unload here. More the chance of a brief text than a late-night phone call, and nothing's off limits, so long as it's frothy, funny or otherwise marks a personal or cultural spot in the book of Jack and Laurie.

All kinds of online friends from school and university, footy, basketball and cricket. Those writers with whom I've walked a shared path, from Ethan to Michelle, and so many others, here, over east, and around the world.

And there's Dash. In recent times, the lockdown seems to have been exclusively designed to settled long-held debates, such as whether my mum deliberately unplugged the Sega Mega Drive when Dash was just about to break my *Bulls vs Lakers* winning streak; if it's true that Trent, with permanent marker in hand, once tried to tag a moving train; why, exactly, I was banned from assemblies as a prefect in second semester, when it was clear I'd been going down a storm with the student population.

It's still sometimes lonely, most often at night, and that's something I'll need to work on. Acceptance of time on my own, late into the night. Acknowledgement that I'm enough, in track pants and a tee, eating berries from a bowl. Really, it's worth celebrating, rather than shaming, a father and author who chose to be both because he sought a greater connection to the world and to the people around him. That's less the story of a lonely guy and more the story of a man who now fundamentally knows that he wants to be embedded in the lives of those he loves, and who love him.

Part of being alone is sitting with not only who you are, but who you've been at other times. That's the lesser-discussed aspect to personal growth. You don't just replay you winning the flag, or being broadcast on the BBC, over and over. You look at the parts of you long denied or forgotten. The times you played small, why you did it, and how you might welcome those younger versions of you into the room, with all their flaws and shortcomings.

Now with two boys of my own, I do things I could and maybe should have done a long time ago. I apologise to some boys from high school who at the time I saw as weak, and upon whom I took out my frustrations, projecting my hurt as quick wit, and cutting comments. Really, I was just a heartbroken kid, a cynic, too young, and sometimes, a bit of a dick.

So I apologise.

*Don't mention it*, says one.

*It's forgotten*, says another.

*You hurt me*, says another. *I remember when you did that. It hurt me at the time. I'm glad you finally found the strength to say you're sorry.*

Being a dad is challenging in that it's easy to remain a boy in a man's body and be a certain kind of a dad – one who still has nights out with the boys, and regular weekends down south or up north, away from the demands of parenthood, and the noise of the family home. But it's much more challenging to show up and sit with a child's, or your own, discomfort.

Are you lonely? I want to ask Noah. *Me too.*

Do you get sad sometimes and you don't know why? *I do.*

How do I do this right? *I'm not sure. Let's find out together.*

# Music

We've bought a wireless, portable speaker for our home in place of a larger home stereo, and what in previous homes would be a living room centrepiece. At first, it felt so strangely alien. This tiny speaker with a goal to somehow fill our house with sound the way my Kenwood did back in the nineties when the biggest decision concerning my disposable income was which CD to buy, and which tracks to play, over and over.

I'm not sure why we went the portable option. While we often head out to playgrounds or parks, the thought of any of us sitting still for long enough to listen to music is ridiculous. Still, it looks good, and sounds pretty good for something roughly the size of a paperback novel.

Annaya says music is our family's central motif, the thing that brings us all together. She's owned two albums in her life, though, so she's not exactly Myf Warhurst. If we're tired, or the boys are listless, we put on some songs to get them moving, and to give us a second's rest.

As for what we play, well, that's a greater bone of contention. Noah likes mostly pop music. He didn't always, but then sure enough, while I was away for work on the East Coast, *things* started happening. A stray Dua Lipa track was added to his playlist. His school was already ushering him into Katy Perry, Taylor Swift and BTS.

I let it slide for a while, a bit like a father saying, 'Take *one*,' when offering up a bowl of lollies. I'd hoped that he'd hear these songs and find them too sweet. On some level, I also didn't want to be too prescriptive in that music is meant to be enjoyed, a personal journey of self-discovery.

It's the surfacing of a strange conundrum, and a reminder to never overtly judge Noah or his musical preferences. And yet, I'd still rather have smallpox than listen to the majority of today's pop songs, many of which he loves, and loves to listen to.

And so, that morning, as I get ready for work, I talk through my worries with Annaya.

'Do I need to play him The Smiths?' I ask her.

'The Smiths?'

'As a means of introduction,' I say. 'A way of bonding with like-minded kids.'

'So, he'll need to find some six-year-olds who love maudlin, depressing music.'

'You know what I mean.'

'Not really,' she says.

I tell her music is currency. That, when I was a teenager, we could talk about the albums we liked, and even listened to them in the school library.

'So what did you listen to?'

'Run DMC, They Might Be Giants. Faith No More. We played *Angel Dust* so much we nearly wore out the CD.'

'So when did The Smiths get involved?'

'Oh, like never,' I say. 'I got into them in my twenties after my first big break-up. I was feeling melancholy and needed some "woe is me" to counteract Perth's perpetual, ever-mocking sunny disposition.'

'And this is good for Noah how?'

'What do you mean?'

'I mean he's not a teenager, he's just a kid,' says Annaya. 'He doesn't need to be Richard Kingsmill yet, or ever for that matter. He just needs to find music he loves. Like you did, remember?'

I loved all kinds of music as a kid, and I'm probably the only kid ever who got in trouble for singing 'Invisible Touch' in the playground, and 'A Spoonful of Sugar' during class. For me, music *was* my emotional register. I could cheer along to 'The Stroke' by Billy Squire, not really knowing what it meant, or segue effortlessly into a sad, reflective state just from the opening bars of 'At Seventeen'. At the same time, there was always the suggestion that at some point I'd need to commit to heavier stuff. Ultimately, your teenage years were to be pummelled into submission rather than felt. You could get away with Jane's Addiction or the Stone Temple Pilots but were better playing Rage Against the Machine. They'd let you off with Pearl Jam, who were at times deeply introspective but rocked out often enough to hide the fact. To us, they were a shared catharsis, an invitation to get more deeply in touch with our emotions. We bonded together with this band both vulnerable and at the same time, necessarily resilient, knowing that in those lyrics they were implicitly saying, 'Hey man, it's okay. You're meant to feel things in this world.'

I go to the library a bit out of sorts. I revisit the bands of my youth, some of whom I still love, and without whom I would have struggled to articulate the angry, sad, or otherwise maligned parts of me. A quieter voice, and one I often pushed down in my teenage years, says we love Peter Gabriel and Natalie Merchant too, and man, one time in your early twenties, you just put on a beanie, cranked up *Teaser* and *The Firecat*, and sang and fake-strummed to the whole album. It was funny, and awesome, and even kind of beautiful when you sang 'Moonshadow' and I saw something I'd not seen in you for a very long time.

As the day progresses, irrational thoughts begin to surface. Not so much, *Have I left the oven on?* as *What if Noah listens to Flo Rida?* I fret he'll hear 'Blurred Lines' and not want to knee Thicke in the nuts or will bop along to LMFAO and never once go, 'Hang on, these guys are total dickheads!'

With some trepidation, I re-enter the house at around four pm, put my keys on the ring, and hear 'Dynamite', Taio Cruz's ode to capitalism and late-night drinking establishments, blaring out of the portable speaker.

I enter the living room, ready to leap tables, to bounce off couches, to do anything to shut off this mix of elation and brand recognition. It's crazily overproduced. I mean seriously, he sounds like he's singing from inside a data centre. Then I see my boy: it's the bridge, and he's bopping out of control, feeling every note.

At that moment, the song is irrelevant but important all at once. I mean, not in terms of all the product placement and all that status nonsense. In those tiny bits of joy, though, it's clear the song's connecting with Noah. He is no longer the shy kid, eyes down, scared of being seen. This is his heart, his tiny soul dancing with abandon, free to shine in the space, and be wild, crazy, free.

When the bass next drops, I pretend I'm playing the keyboard part and burst into the room, arms left, right, up, and down. My legs aren't doing much, they're rooted to the ground from years of paralysis at the thought of dancing, but they're bending nonetheless, and I stretch out at the sight of my boy, feeling the music.

'We're dancing!' he says.

'Woo!'

We synchronise movement, with matching twin-kicks, legs in, and then I lift him, swirling around in a circle, his legs bobbing up and down from the motion until again I drop him down, I spin him around, put my hand on his hips, and we train a circle around the room. We start off locomotive but then move into a conga kick, *da da da da da-dah!*, again and again. Suddenly, I love this song, I mean seriously, I fucking love it, and a part of me – that part that always has to be right, dies.

The song finishes, and I'm exhausted, with him on one side of the room and me on the other. I think we're done, but Noah's up; he's ready to go. 'Again!' he says.

'Once more.' He smirks as if he knows there's no way that we'll stop at one. '*Once*.'

I hit repeat, and the beat hits. I lean back. He puts his right foot back, bends down as if about to start a race. I brace myself, and then he runs. I lift him, swinging him around and around, and then back down. We're in, out, around, into a conga kick, down to some weird-arse arm jiggle, into a crazy-cuddle half dance, and then he laughs, and I laugh, and I don't know *what* this song is, and I hope it never stops.

# LETTING GO

## Red Sun

Things get worse before they get better. *Greater City Shadows*, my mostly respected but as yet unpublished book, continues to raise eyebrows across Australia. In his email response, Declan, a long-time friend and now publisher, wonders why I am trying so desperately hard in my work to not be funny.

He says my genre of choice, short stories, is only slightly less popular than Clive Palmer. He tells me I need to snap out of the notion that publishers are curators when really, they're suppliers to bookstores.

Declan's rejection hurts more than most as we used to work together all the time. Only now he wants the old me back; that early writer, who, in 2005, would never have used literary trickery in the place of a good old-fashioned yarn.

*But you told me to write a great book*, I keep thinking, recalling a conversation we'd had years earlier in a cafe in Fitzroy he most likely barely remembers.

*It's no one's fault, it's just something that happened*, says a voice that's calmer and kinder. It's like the voice I find when lying next to Noah as we stare up at his galaxy of glow-in-the-dark stars.

*What will you do?* this new voice asks.

I don't know.

*Shall we find out?*

Okay.

And like that, the voice remains. It listens and acknowledges.

Are you real? I ask the voice.

*Yes.*

What do you want?

*I want you to be happy.*

You don't want me to be excellent?

*Be excellent if you want, and I'll love you either way. You're a person, not an exam result.*

I pause. Where were you?

*I was here the whole time. Only you didn't want to listen.*

Via a follow-up email, I thank Declan for his response. I say, 'One day I'll write a book you will love, and then you'll be sorry.'

With all this chaos, and all this loss, a fellow award-winning writer, philosopher, and long-time friend agrees to read *Greater City Shadows.* After reading it, she says, 'Maybe you need to sit on this one for a bit.'

In a couple of the stories, she asks, 'Why?' She's being specific according to each instance in the work, but in my head, it's a more general, 'Why?', as in:

- Why are you so obsessed with writing short stories despite your debut novel being relatively well received?
- Why is everything you write filled with so much longing? Why can't you just be despondent, or coolly detached?

- Why do you always put the degree of difficulty so high for the things you write? Why not just tell a story from A to B?

I can't answer any of those questions. I tell her the 'why' for one of the stories she's queried; that there's this song sung in Cantonese, and I'm not sure why, but it really touched me. I tell her she should listen to it; it's called 'Red Sun' (紅日).

'What's it about?' she asks, and I realise I don't know.

I first listened to 'Red Sun' – as recorded in 1992 by Hacken Lee – while researching a story. The moment the song began, I felt as though I was about to set sail on a pirate ship. I listened again and was again immediately geed-up in a way I'd not been since hearing 'St Elmo's Fire (Man in Motion)', as an eight-year-old.

That 'Red Sun' resonated with me made little to no sense. I was clearly depressed, completely lost, and yet the words, spoken in a language different to my own, felt heartening. Each time I heard it, the song rekindled my strength, resilience, and sense of hope in the face of defeat.

My inner critic *hated* this. It said, *I have any number of Tool albums and some System of a Down next-level shit for when you're ready to face reality.*

Instead, I looked up the English translation of the lyrics to 'Red Sun'. The song read like a how-to guide to life for the lost, lonely or afraid. Indeed, the song had felt so inspiring because the lyrics, in whatever language, had turned out to be just as inspiring.

The main messages from the music and lyrics, as decoded by multiple listens and reading the translation of Lee's original lyrics seemed as follows:

*Life is a struggle.*
*Things will at times feel unbearably hard.*
*Nothing of any worth can come without pain and great sacrifice.*

I still believe much of this to be true. And, in the years prior, I'd often talked to emerging writers about the importance of solace: how an exquisite story or honest, vulnerable essay can give one genuine hope, whatever its response in the greater world, and eventually lead one back to the light.

I'd always thought that success with one's writing was a matter of excellence, wherein an author chooses the perfect words, and searches for the most insightful metaphor, and never stops working on a piece until it's clear they've drawn all the blood they possibly can from that particular stone.

Perhaps in more recent times, my definition of excellence has become increasingly limiting. Over time, I've drawn a tiny frame around the concept, squeezing life out of my practice, for fear that Laurie the person – as opposed to Laurie the author – might walk in and screw it all up.

'Red Sun' seems to challenge that line of thinking. Having read the translated lyrics, I feel not so much educated as acknowledged. I sit in that complexity, my certainty evaporating each day, replaced by a sense of solace and some greater, likely unanswerable, questions about life'.

What am I meant to be doing in my limited time on this earth? What one thing could I do that might leave my mark, and help others, all at once?

*We don't know*, says a voice I think at first is my inner critic. Then I realise, in its warmth, that it's the new voice, laughing as it speaks. *We're not supposed to know, and you don't have to know yet or ever, and that will still be fine with me.*

I introduce 'Red Sun' to my boys, first on the wi-fi speaker, and then with the accompanying video clip. They love both; after, we act out the mishaps befallen to Hacken Lee in the clip: a bucket of water in the face. A woman kissing his cheek. A puppy! Howling winds. A boxing glove to the cheek. An egg to the forehead. A towel to wipe it off.

There's a section towards the end where Hacken is thrust into traffic, his arms tied to a log that sits upon his shoulders. He tries to cross the road but keeps getting in other people's way, and eventually he sits down on the kerb, disconsolate.

When I ask the boys their favourite part of the video, Josh says it's this exact moment. 'That's Daddy,' he says. 'That's you.'

At my desk that night, the kinder, calmer voice returns.

*What will you write next?* asks my inner sage.

I don't know. How do you know?

I *don't know*, it says. *Let's go find out.*

The days bleed into school drop-offs and pick-ups, coffee and berry granitas with one boy and a muffin with the other, depending on the day. Throughout, Annaya reminds me that *Greater City Shadows* is impressively stuck, gently suggesting that if you come across a dead cat on the side of the road, you don't try to revive it. You move on.

'But what about the cat?'

'It's gone,' she says. 'Believe me, you did everything you could.'

I meet up again with my friend Mish, and it's like a harrowing episode of Dr. Phil. Two writers, with her on the way up, and me one rejection away from becoming a street performer.

Michelle had been in a similar spot with her writing prior to now and had handled things with much greater grace and decorum over a much longer period of time. In that same place, I'm at a loss. I text her each rejection as if to say, 'Can you please stop this happening?'

She's flying with her own writing, due to be published later that year. She tells me to start something new. To write about my life as it is now. She says I can send out single stories in the meantime, which to me feels like a consolation prize, or a participation trophy.

My inner critic never sleeps, it seems, and so even as the new voice defends the merit of new work, somewhere between pick-up and drop-off, my inner critic reminds me not to listen to anyone other than them, as no one else can be trusted to have my back and get me through a crisis.

I make a promise to myself. I promise to keep writing, only this time in my own voice, about my life. I don't know how these words will come, or when. I try, then delete what's written on the screen. I go again and hate the way in which the words come together.

I pray to Hacken Lee, playing 'Red Sun', over and over, slowly surrendering to the things I don't yet know.

It's early morning when Noah takes me by my hand and guides me to my study. It's been months, maybe a year since people have started telling me they do not want to publish Greater City Shadows.

'I've been thinking,' he says, 'about you being sad. Maybe you could write a story about you and me.'

'You and me?' I say. The first part sounds fine, the second infinitely challenging.

He nods. 'The things we do, the games we play. Maybe we make a joke sometimes. Or I dance, and you lift me up high, and then I touch the sky.'

'Okay, sweetheart,' I say. 'Give me a hug.'

He hugs me, this time in a sit-down hug, my personal favourite on account of a bad back, and the growing boy he's fast become.

He walks across to my whiteboard. Takes the red marker and pops the lid.

He stretches up to the only spot he can reach and writes 'True stories of my life' in a fluid, simple scrawl. He puts the lid back on the pen, drops it back onto the shelf.

'Like that?' I say.

'Like that,' he says, and walks out of the room.

## Last Time

When Josh was born, with downy hair on his back, and his smudgy, kissable face, I fell in love all over again. It was the first time I realised what my mum meant when she'd said that you love each child in different ways. The amount of love, of course, is the same; it's the means by which that love is shared or communicated that is different.

Initially, Josh fitted in my arms like a cobloaf, and when he grew bigger, he scampered round the house like a tiny, doughy puppy of a boy. Some nights, as he slept, I would gently touch his cheek. Sometimes, he would stir and I would scarper, quick as a flash, thinking, *No, no, please don't wake up!*

While an unexpected break from my PhD meant much time with Noah as a newborn, time with Josh at that same stage was harder to find. When I finished my contract in the public service, though, we decided to make up for lost time and started a new tradition: Daddy–Josh day, every Friday.

While working in government, time with Josh came only when I was at my most tired, and in need of a rest. This naturally affected how present I was with him, and how willing I was to take part in what might otherwise have been an enjoyable or rewarding moment. I did my best, of course, but even so I knew that what we had in our Daddy–Josh days was something special.

This new tradition of bonding spanned two years while I set

up my business. We've had breakfasts together, we've shared cakes and babycinos, we've badly flung frisbees and kicked soccer balls to all corners of the local parks, and I've carried him more than he walked, rationalising how he's probably tired, knowing all the while that I just as much wanted to see his face light up as I lifted him up, and into my arms.

Unfortunately, I still need to help pay the bills, though. While business is good, my workload's at the point where I'll need to go full-time, just to keep up. I talked about this with Josh earlier in the week. How he'll now go to Nan and Pops on Fridays, and to think of all the fun they'll have together. He seemed to understand. At the time, the decision made sense for us both, and maybe soon enough we can revert to a four-day work week and a Friday that's more fun than frustrating. For the time being, though, this Friday marks our last Daddy–Josh Day.

We're checking out Croc's, the new kids play centre in our area. It opens at nine, and I keep myself busy the morning of the Croc's visit. I unload and reload the dishwasher, pack Noah's school bag, check my emails, and put on a Dog Man audiobook to keep the boys entertained in the lead-up to drop-off time.

We drop Noah at the school gate, then take a quick trip north on the Mitchell Freeway and on to Croc's. It's an emporium of fun, with three different themed party-rooms, two bouncy castles, some weird cage thing that looks like it's left over from a Nickelodeon game show and a smaller cage/mesh mess that is the type of place your kids would climb into and then invariably get stuck.

'What do you want to do?' I ask Josh.

He says, 'Muffin,' and points to the cafe.

At this point, muffins are very much off-limits for me as are most other sweet treats since I started going to the gym. As for how it's going, well, it's been interesting. Only a few months into my health kick, they closed the gyms, and so from there I worked out in my study, really not more than a box with a desk, until they reopened. And so, instead of indulging in some sweet craving, I get a coffee, my last remaining vice and way to stay awake for my parenting duties.

We take his muffin, my water, and an apple and blackcurrant pop-top, and walk to the table, my steps shortened to align with Josh's tiny strides. Then we sit down at a wobbly metal table, our seat legs scraping on the concrete floor.

'Hey Josh,' I say. 'Check out the bouncy castle!'

'This is not the same as the bouncy castle we went to in Busselton, right?'

'Correct.'

'You were writing a story this morning,' he says, smiling. 'What was it about?'

'Oh, you mean that one set in the Swan River?' I ask. 'It's about a guy and a fish.'

'A funny fish?'

'Well kind of, I mean, he used to be funny,' I say, and reach for a fragment of muffin.

Josh casts a suspicious glance. 'What are you doing?'

'I'm having some muffin.'

'No, no,' he says. 'You're not allowed to have muffin.'

'Well, what am I going to do?'

'You have your coffee,' he says, and then perks up, in full customer-service mode. 'There you go, sir. Your soy flat white!'

We eat – or should I say, *he* eats – as we sit there silently. I look around and it seems everyone has a sweet muffin apart from me. But then, I did have many a sweet muffin in the past twenty years. And that, most likely, is why it's imperative for me to move on from a muffin-based diet into one that respects five food groups.

I ask Josh which Wiggle he likes the most, and he says Simon because red is his favourite colour. I tell him there's a brown and an orange Wiggle too, and he thinks I'm joking, and for a second I wonder if I dreamed that, because after a while all the Wiggles episodes bleed into each other. I realise then I'm talking to my second son about something I saw while raising my first. I'm not sure why but having two kids often brings a strange echo into proceedings. Looking down at Josh's tiny light-up sneakers resting alongside mine – you're not allowed to wear shoes when on play centre equipment – I think back to Noah's similarly once-minute thongs.

'Hey, what's your favourite memory of our Fridays together?'

Josh smiles. 'I don't know.'

'You're not sure?'

'I don't know,' he repeats, and takes a sip of his pop-top.

My favourite memory has nothing to do with the places we've been. It's the combined memories of my time with Josh.

His joyous, heartfelt smile. His unending curiosity. How happy he is to just sit, cuddle or play with me. His ability to tell me what he's feeling, even at this young age, knowing all the while that I'll be able to help.

We finish our drinks and head into the main area. I duck down, heading through a door of plastic strips and lifting Josh over the bump. Once inside, we throw foam balls at each other, and then feed a machine with armfuls of those same blue, pink, green and yellow balls, but in much greater numbers. The balls travel up pipes to a giant basket above our heads. It takes forever to fill it up, but once we do, we hit a button, an alarm sounds, and for a second it's raining multicoloured globes of foam and we shout out in glee.

I take Josh on a go-kart on an otherwise empty track. We circle, over and over, and I see a smile spread wide across his face. We play one of those crane games where they pretend you might win a cuddly toy. I line up the crane with expert precision, even going to the side of the machine to make sure it's in the perfect position. I lower it, and it's perfect, stretching its hand out and then in, to pick up a giant cuddly Minion from the movie *Despicable Me* but then as it raises, it just kind of massages the Minion on its way up, and we're done, and Josh is okay with it, but I am gutted, as I wanted something tangible for him to take away from our time together. Something soft and warm, that reminds him he's in my heart, and on my mind, even when I'm not with him.

We head back to the table.

'You want another muffin?' He shakes his head. 'A drink?'

'No.'

'We can play again if you want.'

'No, let's talk,' says Josh. 'In *Dog Man Unleashed*, Dog Man and the chief catch the bad guy. Petey is the bad guy. There's Li'l Petey too, but he's not the bad guy.'

'Cool. Who's the other bad guy? Is that Flippy?'

'No, Flippy's a good guy. Remember? He was a bad guy, then he turned good. It's in *A Tale of Two Kitties*.'

In that moment, my son is doing better than me with a complex array of feelings. I'm hoping that's because we've done enough to have him feeling loved, valued, and appreciated. In my head, there's this adult voice that calmly explains why I need to go full-time, at least for a bit. And yet, underneath that, there's an adult voice that knows this time is not only sacred, but distressingly finite. That I may look back on and cherish these memories with Josh, and that, while I'll be able to remember a manuscript I assessed in similar detail, the feelings won't be nearly as rich, or long-lasting.

It's a strange thing to have come full circle around needing to get by, and wanting to be present. And, maybe this time, because the work feeds into my passion, rather than dampening it down, I might be able to work and play with equal levels of commitment.

Time will tell. All I know right now is that I'm sad to have reached this moment, and that I wish we could have one more, as I'm torn between being the kind of dad that provides for his family, and the one who just wants to spend as much time as he can with them.

As we leave the play centre and walk back to the car, I ask Josh if he enjoyed himself today. Whether he liked the go-karts best, or the ball room, or bouncing on the trampoline. He doesn't answer straight away. When he does, he says, 'I don't know. I just love my Daddy–Josh days.'

# Tiny, Fragile Hearts

I'm on the last day of teaching a weekend writing retreat in the Perth Hills when I receive a text from Alice. It says: Your father is in an ambulance. *He's had a heart attack and is heading to the hospital.*

Alice and Dad had been splitting up in the weeks leading up to the heart attack. She had wanted to move down south, and Dad was keen to stay in York. That's the official story; I think in the aftermath of Dad's accident in 2013, she'd been involuntarily thrust into becoming Dad's carer, as opposed to his wife, and this took a toll on her and their relationship in the years that followed.

When she messaged me, I figured it was something to do with that, not that his heart had simply stopped in the face of marital heartbreak.

As with the last time, they have to first get Dad to Northam, and then transfer him to Royal Perth Hospital. And so I text back, saying I'll see them at Royal Perth either tonight or tomorrow, depending on what happens from here, and then head into the house, to teach three writing hopefuls.

The final spot of that day is where a now established writer comes in to talk to the participants about reaching publication. That day, I'm grateful for a one-time student and now debut author, Caleb, to be back here, smiling, proud and full of energy. He hands them each a notebook, all especially selected and personally inscribed. He talks about his journey as though it were the making of him, when I know it was at times also the damn-near breaking of him.

I check my texts when I go to the toilet in case something, or indeed anything, has happened. I go to the toilet more than usual that day, but the updates are sketchy, impossible to follow. I know he's being transferred to Perth at some point, but nothing other than that, not even an estimated time of arrival.

When it's time to go home, rain's pouring from the sky, so I drive more slowly and more carefully than usual, taking my time, and waiting for news, when it comes.

I go to Royal Perth Hospital the next day, a Monday. My dad wakes on my arrival and looks terrible. He seems a little out of it, too, and so we talk as though he's suffering from exhaustion, rather than a heart attack.

On Tuesday, Eve arrives, and then Luke, and the doctors say they're going to try to unblock the artery. They tell us this in a room with no natural light, and two couches squeezed into the space to face each other. In terms of COVID protocols, it's a nightmare, but I guess right now that's not their greatest concern.

They say Dad's alcohol and dietary choices have weakened his heart, and that smoking in his youth also did damage. One doctor keeps using this word, weak, and I wonder if our hearts are simply a conglomeration of weaknesses, from loving too much, to needing breath at the top of an ascent. I think of all the coffee I drink, and the peanut butter, cheese and Pizza Shape sandwiches I ate as a teen.

The doctor continues talking about my dad's weak heart. He asks if we have any questions. I say, 'No, but please, be careful.'

He gives us percentages on the dangers of this type of surgery. As numbers go, they're not that bad. They'd be much better, of course, were they not pertaining to the chances of my father dying while he's in the operating theatre.

I make a silent pact: *I'll get you out of here, Dad. However we do it, I am not leaving here without you.*

On Wednesday, I grab two coffees, one for me, and one for Dad, as though it's a quick catch-up on the Terrace as opposed to my navigating the labyrinthine tunnels and cul-de-sacs of Royal Perth Hospital.

We talk extensively about what needs to be done, and get updates, though in truth, it's all for show, as there are extenuating circumstances on the back of Dad's head injuries in 2013, and Alice has power of attorney. I talk to the nurses regardless, and thank them, and badger the doctors when and if I can find them.

And then, after what seems an aeon, they schedule dad's surgery for the Thursday. Alice lets me know, although the announcement comes only an hour or two after the hospital told us it would be happening on Saturday. This happens all the time in this hospital: one doctor says Friday, and another says Monday. They say they're scheduling one medication and then a different one is administered.

But still, we find our way to operation day. Eve has already driven back to Albany, hours away from here, as she was told the operation would be later in the week. Luke is working, Trent continues to be persona non grata with the rest of the family, and Alice does not like driving into the city. So, in the end, it's just me and my dad this time around.

I head in earlier than usual, pull into that same multistorey, 'you could murder someone here and get away with it' carpark. Take the same walkway, always signing in and getting the necessary sticker, taking bridge after bridge – I swear, it's like Madison County in this place – because they built two hospitals in one, but on opposite sides of the road.

I get to Dad, who immediately hands me a lined yellow notepad. He's written things down. There's all kinds of stuff: bank account details, email addresses and passwords. I see the list, and think, *That can't be the sum and total of my dad's life, these numbers and words*, when my world is tied to this man, it rests within his soul, and the memories we've shared.

He tells me what to do with the list, and with his stuff if things goes south. I say, 'They won't,' almost too quickly, and he smiles.

'But if they do,' he says, 'You need to be prepared.'

He sits back on his bed. I sit next to him on the bed, take his palm in mine.

'Hey, Dad.'

'Hmm?'

'I'm scared.'

'Me too,' he says.

Early on, they tell us they'll be operating in the afternoon. In the end, Dad tells me to head down to the cafe, or into the CBD, or anywhere really, to give him and me a break. I walk the streets, tracking every avenue, the corners, shops and traffic conditions, a walking Google Maps.

As time stretches out, I keep walking. Stopping to look at bread, marvelling at the perfect loaves, leavened, raised so fresh, and so delicious. I see a statue in the Hay Street Mall. It commemorates Percy Buttons, one of the city's best-known street entertainers from the 1930s. He was known for his somersaults, tumbles, and handstands. He was mainly a vagrant, but something about Percy struck a chord with Perth, so he was immortalised, mid-handstand, as a show of appreciation. Staring down at Percy, the thought strikes me that Perth is defined not by landmarks but by people. At that point, I'm glad my parents moved here as opposed to anywhere else. It's not a bad place to build a life or a family.

Once I've walked from East Perth to West, I ring Annaya, ask her to come in and have lunch with me.

We eat burgers at Hibernian Place like teenagers, and she lets me talk about how much I love my dad. I tell her stories I've told her before. I express frustration at the old bugger, as if now's the right time to be pissed off about things.

'Big day,' says Annaya. 'You okay?'

I nod. 'If he goes—'

'He'll be okay,' she says, and I know she only says it because that's what you're supposed to say, but I'm still glad she says it.

'Better get back,' I say, but don't get off of my seat.

'Love you,' she says, and again it's time, so we hug, and then she has to go, and so do I, back to the tunnels I've called home for these past few days.

The operation takes five and a half hours. I go downstairs for a bit, only checking in with the ward once the first two hours have passed. I do this as a stopgap, as before that point, I'm replying to texts from my various family members saying *nothing yet*. I go back to the ward, and they tell me, 'Nothing yet,' so I head back down to the cafe.

I call Annaya. I tell her, 'Nothing yet.' I call my friend Dash and we talk about hip-hop and the NBA. He says he's pretty sure the Sixers will go all the way this year, so long as Simmons brings his A-game. I ask if he's talking about the same team that's been applying 'The Process' for years and getting diddly squat back.

He laughs, says, 'Yes, I am talking about that same team, you piece of shit.'

We laugh, and then fall silent. I say, 'I'm scared. Like, really fucking scared.'

A pause. 'I would be too, man. It's huge, you know?'

He tells me it's a beautiful thing when you can be there for somebody you love. I say, 'Thanks, man' and end the call as quickly as I can as I'm about to bawl my eyes out.

I text my sister Eve: *Nothing yet*. I head upstairs to the ward, and again they tell me, 'Nothing yet.'

Throughout this time, I talk to my dad in my head and say, You okay, old man? And every time, I hear a yes. I hold onto those yeses until it's almost a parlour game, call and response, and I'm waiting for him to yell, 'YES! For Christ's sake, yes!' but he never does, he's so amazingly calm inside my anxious head.

At five pm, four hours after surgery began, they tell me he's still in theatre. I sit upstairs in a hallway immediately outside the operating theatre from that point on. I pray, over and over, although I'm pretty sure God says, 'Oh, so now I'm your god. Tell me, heathen, what exactly is it that you need?'

*I need your help. Not for me, it's for my father. Also, I'm sorry I've never believed you exist. To be honest, I still don't.*

*Then why talk to me now?*

*I'm desperate. I'm scared. I cannot bear to think of a life without my dad.*

The doctor comes out. He says Dad's still in the operating theatre, only this time he gives me more information. I mishear most of it, because he seems anxious, so I'm anxious as well. What I can establish is that they're still trying to unblock the artery. I check I've got this right, and he says, 'Yes.'

He also says they'll have to call it off if they can't clear the blockage.

From there, I watch the clock. I text *nothing yet* to Luke and Eve. I call Dash. He tells me about this time Derek Harper held onto the ball when he should have shot it. How a few games later, he took the shot that time and won the game.

I ask him what that has to do with the Philadelphia 76ers.

He says, 'Nothing. It's just a cool story.'

I pause. 'I love you, man.'

He says, 'I love you too. But you know you are a clown sometimes.'

'You know it,' I say. 'Clown.'

I pray some more, think maybe God is us, all this love, and all these people wanting others to be happy. Every friend we've ever met, dreamed up specifically to bring our days to life. And then I think about the time I yelled at Dad after I returned from the east coast of Australia in the aftermath of a particularly painful break-up.

I told him he didn't understand. That he could not possibly know what it was like to be in such pain. That I needed him, right now, and why couldn't he just be there for me?

He looked back at me, clearly hurt, but his eyes still filled with love, and he said, 'I welcomed you here, I sat with you. I'm here with you right now as you're yelling at me. I think I understand.'

It can be hard to reconcile the inherent selfishness of being a son. And so, while I'm petrified, I'm also happy to be there for him, and perhaps, to understand him as he once understood me, in my time of need.

The doors open, and the orderlies are smiling. He's there, my dad, he's actually there, I can see him, and he lifts his head up and smiles. He gives the thumbs up, and I leap up, take his hand in mine, and they say they have to go. Still, I jog alongside him for the run of the hallway, and then he's gone again, and I can't stop smiling.

The head surgeon comes out, and tells me they couldn't unblock the artery. In my head, I think that means they didn't *finish* unblocking the artery, and so after a bit of back and forth where it seems that neither of us understands the other, I simply say, 'Can you please just tell me he's okay?'

'He's okay,' says the surgeon, and I fall back into the chair, tears streaming down my face, and he hugs me somewhat awkwardly, even as I'm still sitting, and then he leaves, unsure of why I'm so happy that they couldn't do what they had planned to do.

I call Alice and say, 'He's okay.' Call my sister, say, 'He's okay.' Call my brother, say, 'He's okay.' Call Dash and say, 'He made it. Holy shit, he actually made it.'

My heart is made until I go to the ward, walk in, and hug my dad, say, 'Oh, Dad, I'm so glad you're okay.'

The nurse pulls a face. 'It didn't work,' she says.

'What do you mean?' I say.

'They couldn't do it,' she says.

'But they were working at unblocking it, right? I mean, they unblocked some of it?'

She looks at me like I'm crazy, picks up a pencil, and bangs it over and over against her hand. 'They couldn't break it,' she says, with her emphasis on the word 'break', so that what she's saying feels more forceful than intended.

'But he's better.'

'No, he's not better. You have to take out the blockage.'

I ask if I can talk to someone else and she nods. She leaves, and again it's my father and me. He says, 'Oh dear,' and laughs, and I say, 'Dad, it's not funny,' but he keeps laughing, even as he coughs a little too.

A doctor arrives and confirms that in five hours of surgery, precisely nothing was done to change Dad's condition. I check again that I'm hearing him right. He confirms this, apologises, and then leaves the room.

All day, I thought about two different scenarios, and prepared myself for one or the other. Except, it turns out there was a third scenario. Dad was operated on for hours and came out with nothing having changed in the slightest way.

I say, 'This sucks!'

'I'm not particularly happy about it,' says Dad.

'So they didn't do it.'

'They didn't do it.'

'So, what do we do?' I ask.

'The saga continues,' he says, laughing, and I thrust my head in my hands, and think, *No jokes, Dad. Not today.*

## Decadence

In the latter months of 2020, it is all about my father. He's readmitted to hospital two weeks after his original discharge. He swells up, his eyes seemingly gone to water, and this time it's Eve's turn to take him where he needs to be, which, this time, is Hollywood Hospital, in Perth's inner western suburbs.

I go to see him, and he jokes about sequels, and the food, and what's on TV. They put in a pacemaker, we get him out of there and there's some suggestion of normality. It's a normality that's shattered only weeks later when he's readmitted to hospital.

It feels like I've missed months of my own life during these hospital stays. Were it not for Annaya and the boys, I'd have presumed this was a nightmare, wanting only to keep Dad safe, but continually having to take him back into peril.

When we're not at hospital, Annaya and I wake early, at around five thirty in the morning thanks to Josh's habit of poking both of us until we wake up. We go to bed much later on account of both boys thinking night-time is the right time to eat dinner, have a dance battle, or ask questions not otherwise answered in the daytime.

Parenting is a relentless job. The hours are terrible, and you never catch up on that sleep you lost when they were newborns. You're also up against the greatest amount of 'knowledge' on a subject that's so obviously flawed, restrictive, or impractical.

As parents, Annaya and I work slowly towards equality, although it's closer to shifting a seesaw in tiny increments, rather than keeping it dead level. Women are societally expected to have an affinity with all things domestic. When I take out the rubbish, I'm conditioned to see that as the big win of the week; I almost raise my hand in acknowledgement to the non-existent crowd to celebrate how I manoeuvred these three coloured bins from the side of the house to the footpath.

Our domesticity, it seems, is so often accentuated by a crash or smash. Annaya buys a slow cooker, and I break the glass lid. I buy a slow cooker; she breaks the glass lid. 'It's not our fault,' I tell her. 'It's at the bottom of the cupboard, below the pots, the pans and the big blender.'

Annaya and I are two very different people who smooth out each other's bumps. A chance meeting from 2007 turned into a life together. A wedding in 2010 turned into two years together, with one child soon after that, and then another, and soon enough my life was simply the days after I met her, all my moments of note falling in and around our family home.

In more recent times, I've spent too much time away from that home. So, it's some surprise when my dad is finally out of hospital, at least for now, and Annaya and I have reached our tenth wedding anniversary.

A special day, turned into a decade, and it's real love, and yet it feels fragile even now, this choice we made. To open up, to be each other's rock, as best we can through love, marriage, our fathers' ailing hearts, and on into parenthood.

In the present day, we make another choice: to reconnect with one another and rekindle the relationship, fanning embers still ready to ignite under the right conditions.

Today we get up early. Dress the kids. Drive them to Nan and Pop's. We've booked a night at a swanky hotel in Perth. Flowers, champagne. I called the concierge earlier and also arranged for chocolates and a series of rose petals that lead from the front door through to the bedroom.

We take two freeways, and soon enough our beaten-up Elantra pulls into a lit-up forecourt, which is likely not the word the hotel uses, but that's exactly what it is. A concierge greets me and says, 'Valet parking?'

'That's right,' I reply. 'It's our tenth anniversary.'

'Congratulations,' he says. 'Just pull in behind the Lamborghini.'

They take our car away, quite possibly to the wrecker, and we enter a foyer like nothing I have ever seen. It's immaculate, with perfectly shined shells hanging on the wall in a wave formation. The ceiling looks tied together by silk; the floor covered with these shiny, glimmering hourglasses.

We wait for an hour to check in, the line nearly reaching the entrance. I get frustrated but then I look again at the walls, and feel immediately soothed, and at one with the surroundings.

Once in our room, we pull back the curtains. Annaya lies on the chaise longue. She's wearing this incredible green-flowing dress. Her hair is out, and flows down, no longer needing to be tied back for the duties of being a mum to two of the most excitable kids in the state.

She looks like a woman I might see and think, *Wow, she's beautiful.* Then she smiles at me, and I am in my own dream. We leave the rose petals on the floor – they're fabric, unfortunately, but more fool me for trying to make a moment happen rather than letting it happen – cuddle up right there on the lounge, looking out at the city I've so struggled with for most of my life. The moments, memories and echoes of years spent in and around those six square kilometres of concrete and glass. My working days just ways to get through to knock-off and my nights spent reading the spoils of a bookshop binge or listening to my latest purchase from Dada or 78 Records.

Seen from here, our city's more striking: no one is ever going to confuse it for New York, Sydney, or Paris, and yet it's when you're away from the CBD, as the river cradles your city, that you see Perth's tiny magnificence. Australia's littlest brother, always trying to act big, never knowing that it's great as it is, not for all it can do but for the space it provides, and the way in which a night at Crown Towers is a big deal for the majority of locals who pretend to live large, if only for the night.

We talk of how the kids would love the pool, and how we should totally bring them here for breakfast. We've heard that the buffet restaurant, The Epicurean, is like a whole continent of food. We talk about an amazing ten years as husband and wife, as we lie in crumpled sheets, and watch the sun dip behind the city's fingertips, those scrapers always built just that little bit higher than the rest of Perth's skyline, as if racing to reach the clouds.

The bath in our hotel room is a risk – we conceived Noah in a very similar bath in Yallingup. She suggests we run it anyway. At first, I want to make love. However, because we are parents, we mostly just want to catch up on some sleep, so after the bath, we hop into bed and close our eyes, taking in the sweet silence and prolonged moments of blessed peace.

When we wake, I turn to Annaya, and she's resting beneath crisp white linen. I kiss her and it's like listening to early Genesis, only better, because while 'Supper's Ready' is an amazing song, it is still not the same as a love that's gone through highs and lows to beat damning statistics on the likelihood of a marriage running its full term. We kiss and though the bed is big, it's not that big that I don't need to be closer to her, so we cuddle up, two people on a massive mattress, and I know that if I opened up the curtains there'd be this amazing view, and an endless sky, but I'm more than happy right here in the dark, with our feet entwined on a Saturday afternoon.

The next morning, we eat at The Epicurean, and it is the first time I've had pretzels for breakfast, and the first time I've had doughnuts for breakfast, and the first time I've had green juice for breakfast, and the first time I've ordered an omelette but not eaten it because I'm too busy staring at my love.

'You remember that time you nearly died?' That was our

honeymoon, 2010, when a trip to Bali sent Annaya's tummy into spasm. We went first to a community hospital, and then a real one, as I imagined myself getting off the plane and having to tell her parents there was nothing we could do.

She nods. 'You remember the time *you* nearly died?' I'd spent the summer in the States, in Iowa, ate one too many pie shakes (you take your favourite piece of cake or sweet pie, and they mix it into a milkshake) and come home to emergency gall-bladder surgery. They had to take it out in the end: a stone had blocked the cystic duct, and the bladder had gone septic.

'How about when Noah fell off at the playground?'

'You remember any good stuff?' I say, laughing.

'I remember all the good stuff. Thanks for being my husband.'

'Thanks for being my wife.'

'And thank you,' she says, 'for loving our boys, and for being a great dad.'

'That's what we do, right?'

'If we can,' she says.

'Well, you're an amazing mum.'

'Ah, I don't know.'

'We don't know, do we? But we try, and we're there, doing the best we can.'

Annaya suggests we book the room for another night, not to stay, but to sleep off breakfast and come back for lunch, but already our time is running out. So we eat our doughnuts, hold each other's hands, head up to the room, and then it's time to check out, and again become parents.

At home, we show our boys the pictures of churros, bacon, bratwurst, all on Annaya's plate as I'm a vegetarian, but I live in a house of cave people, always fawning on the flesh.

'So you went for your wedding anniversary,' says Noah.

'That's right.'

'What was it like, your wedding?'

'It was incredible. You would have loved it.'

'Did you kiss Mummy?'

'Um, yes,' I say. 'A little too much, in fact.'

Noah laughs. 'Maybe one day you'll get married again, and we can be there.'

'Give me a cuddle,' I say. I stand up, waiting for him to get into position, and then lift, first clean, and then jerk, pushing him up, his knees onto my shoulders.

He 'touches the sky', a thing we do where he reaches up, and puts his fingers to the ceiling. First one hand, and then the other, and then I lower him down, pull him close.

'You think we could get married again, me and your mum?' I say.

Noah nods. 'I think you could get married again, you and your ... bum!' he shouts, turning out of my arms, and landing with knees bent. He laughs, and runs away, and in the distance, he's still laughing until he reaches his room.

Annaya catches me smiling. 'What's up with you?'

'No, it's just we're lucky, you know?'

'I know,' she says. 'Only some days, it's brutal.'

'Some days, you just want to yell "Stop!" I say. 'Like, Jesus, are you done with me yet?' Annaya laughs.

'Sometimes, you're hardly there for weeks, even months,' she says, 'and then you hit a point. One day, it's there, all that joy. You haven't earned it, as you wouldn't have noticed a fat fire, you were that tired. But it's there. It's yours. So you take it, feeling dumb, and blessed.'

I pull Annaya in for a hug, and we stay there on the couch for the longest time, as the sun sets and the living room leans into darkness. Still, it's okay. The hallway light is on; hell, I'm not even sure we turned it off from last night, and I hear both boys in the hall, playing, laughing, as we hold on to each other.

# Trick Shot

Noah gets out of bed at six most mornings. I know this because we bought him a day–night clock which is blue through the night, but turns yellow at six, which means no coming in until then. It's the third-term school holidays, so there's little to no pressure to get the kids ready. Still, six o'clock is still early if it's every morning for the foreseeable future. He's clearly an author's son in terms of his foreshadowing. Before arriving, he flicks on the lights, one by one, through the house until he reaches our bedroom.

He's wearing his Star Wars pyjamas, a gift from his auntie Rae, and they were big at the time, but man, Noah could rock an onion sack, such is his undeniable charisma, so Rae was clearly onto something.

Josh comes soon after, wearing Cookie Monster pyjamas. He's still short enough that when he enters a room, we see only a mop of curly hair pass by as he makes his way over to my side of the bed. From there, he just jumps on, a kind of 'see how it goes' approach that usually ends with his foot in my nuts, or a head bump to my nose.

'What time is it?'

'Six oh three.'

It's not 6.03. We put their clocks back ten minutes so we could get a tiny bit more sleep, only it's not helping, it just makes us more tired.

'Daddy, it's trick shots today. And then Mario Kart on Friday, and Dome on Saturday.'

'Cool.'

'And what day is Sunday?'

The day I catch up on bills. The day I do the lawns.

'iPlay!' says Noah and runs out of the room.

'iPlay!' yells Josh and throws his hands in the air. He's lying with his head close to the middle of bed, and then, without provocation, starts to kick at my face from sheer excitement.

I promised them we could go to iPlay, an emporium of video games, ticket machines, and things that go beep in the day. I promised this because I worked the previous weekend teaching writing workshops to a group of emerging WA writers, now green-lit for support and development as part of the Four Centres Emerging Writers' Program. My job was to teach them the essentials of writing; given the option and where I'm currently at in my career, I'm almost tempted to yell, 'Go back! You're crazy, save yourselves!' Except they're not crazy, and I know that they're not crazy, and perhaps one day I'll look back on this time and laugh, seeing that while I was undoubtedly in a valley at the time, it was already leading up to the next peak.

Josh starts screeching for no reason, smiling after each screech as if to say, *Did you see what I just did?* In the kitchen, I hear a plate smash, and Noah yells, 'Uh-oh! Dad, I broke a plate!' A pause. 'I need a bandaid!'

This, or something similar, happens maybe three times a week.

I find Noah, open the bandaid wrapper as carefully as I can. It ends up torn and so begins a tug-of-war between me and the wrapper as to who will get the spoils. I eventually win the tussle, being careful not to step on the shards of plate, and stick the bandaid around the top of Noah's index finger, before kissing the top of his finger and, accidentally, the bandaid too, then lifting him into my arms, which gets harder with each passing year as he's now less of a cub and more a baby giraffe.

While this kind of thing is stressful for me, for Annaya it's not so much a job as a responsibility. Some nights she cries, she just cries, and at the point where I'm like, *What the hell is going on?*, she says, 'I'm worried about Noah,' so I sort my shit out, hold her close, talk her through it as best I can. I know from her tone and her tears that this is not a moment in time; it's a thing she will feel for the rest of her life.

When this happens, I try to actively listen, not able to solve a single thing in that moment but hoping that by being there, I'm hearing the struggle, and validating what it's like for her as a mum.

It's here that I see being a dad and being a mum are fundamentally different roles; or perhaps that's only in relation to our marriage, and it's just greatly different being me, as opposed to Annaya. On a good day, she's 'We Are Family' inclusive, collaborative; the three of them playing board games, doing craft, or dancing to Kidz Bop songs. On a bad day, things still aren't that catastrophic: even when she's struggling, she's level-headed, and good to go if she can get in a nap, or just a chance to wash her hair, and feel closer to revived.

On a bad day, I'm grumpy, irritable and longing for everyone to immediately learn the basics of TV remotes, Nintendo Switch controllers, and wi-fi technology. I get impatient, and at times feel on the brink of cracking the major sads.

On a good day, everything they do is so wonderful and incredible that I can't help telling them I love them, or cuddling them, or wanting to dance like a dickhead with them. It's like hearing 'The Rain, The Park, & Other Things' on Forever Classic 6iX; you figure it won't light you up the way it did the last time, but then it's playing, the raindrop sound effects and the harp glissando, and then the harmonies hit, and you can't help it, the beauty just washes over you, and past, present and future, memories and premonitions all swirl within the one song.

On a good day, I know I'm a great dad. And not only that, but I know I'm closer now than at any other time to contentment and a life well lived. I see that in their faces: I matter so much to them. I am needed, not to win awards, or bring home the bacon, I'm needed here, right now, to be *me*.

By Friday, six am, the dishes have piled up from last night's hodgepodge dinner of ravioli, meatballs and rotis, and there's a litter of breadcrumbs on the kitchen floor. Noah's cradling a foam ball, saying, 'Let's do it, Dad! Let's do *Real Life Trick Shots!*'

*Real Life Trick Shots* is a video starring talented super-sportsmen making impossible tricks in any number of wacky locations such as stores, offices and in their cars, but mostly in their homes. Our trick shots are infinitely more possible than theirs: I'll say, 'This is *Sponge worthy*,' and throw our dish sponge into the sink, or I'll say, 'This is *Mellow Out*,' and lob a marshmallow into a mug from over the kitchen counter.

Lately, Josh has been struggling, as he can't make the shots as consistently as Noah. I can't either, I'm exhausted, but I know that my ability to lob a ping-pong ball into a cup of water is unlikely to decide whether or not my next book gets published, or if I end up making a viable career from my writing.

To be honest, we're all a bit rubbish. I also get the sneaking suspicion the Dude Perfect gang are not quite as all-conquering as they appear to be. Indeed, a quick Google search shows outtakes where they pretty much suck just as bad as we do.

Still, it's hard not to try to excel, as it seems so much of our culture, and particularly masculinity, is benchmarked by performances of undeniable excellence: Dom Sheed's impossible goal for the Eagles in the 2018 Grand Final; Gene Wilder, cane in hand, falling and then somersaulting, before leaping to his feet in *Willie Wonka & The Chocolate Factory*; The White Stripes playing 'Icky Thump' live, and holy shit, is that one person playing two instruments, and both parts, live, for the same song?

I know about excellence. I played football for four seasons on a busted ankle, taping it up before every match. We won a grand final in the end, too, the under seventeens, against West Coast, a kind of all-star team of mostly rich kids from City Beach, Floreat and Wembley Downs.

I told Annaya about it once, as a way of explaining my back story with Jeremy, only even then it still stuck in my throat.

'You want to show me the photos?'

I shook my head.

'Maybe one day,' she said. 'I mean, a win is a win, right?' and I wanted to believe her, but it never felt that way, and indeed it took me years just to want to kick a football again.

On Saturday, Noah asks for pancakes twice. We tell him pancakes aren't a lunchtime food. He says, 'What about chips?' and then pours water onto his plate.

'Noah?'

'My water was not the right water.'

'You keep doing this!' My tone is changing. 'You always—'

Annaya raises an eyebrow, so I try again. 'Noah, we can't just pour water on our plates.'

'No! You're wrong!' I can't not put water on the plate, you can't do that,' he shouts, and runs away from the table, falling hard onto the sitting room couch. I go with him. Easy, easy—

'Noah.'

'You shouted at me!'

'Well, you poured water onto your plate!'

'I didn't.'

'Mate, can you just stop it, now?'

There's a concerned look from Annaya. These looks always feel like she's thinking, *Christ, does he even know what he's doing?*

'Noah, I'm not happy about this. This is not okay. Do you understand? Do you?' And then I notice he's scared. 'Noah.'

He nods but stays silent. 'Noah, baby. Do you want a hug?'

And he does, and so do I.

Later that night, Josh wakes, and I don't know what time it is, but it's crazy late. His nightlight's on, but it's still dark, and I hold him, and I've got him, but my eyes are closing, I'm that shattered.

Josh softens, and it's clear he's about to fall back to sleep. 'I've got you, beautiful boy,' I whisper. He stirs, and I say, 'Shh, shh, shh,' hoping I'll quickly get him back to nodding off.

I pull him up onto my shoulder, and his feet, which are at first clasped around my hips begin to slip down. We dance in tiny circles, pat, pat, shh, shh, shh, and, *You've got this, Laurie. This is why they get you the ball in the final quarter, only a minute left on the clock.*

*You've got this, man. Seal the deal and send it home.*

I wake up tired on the Sunday and Annaya's still sleeping after Josh got her up as well as me, maybe multiple times. Josh is still crashed out too, but Noah comes in nice and early. We snuggle for a bit and then he says, 'Shall we get up?', so I nod and pull on pyjamas and a t-shirt, hit 'on' on the central heating, and head out with him to the kitchen.

Breakfast for me is a two-egg omelette, and for him it's store-bought waffles, toasted and covered in Nutella. At the table, he browses through his album of AFL footy cards.

'Who did you play for, Dad?'

'I played one game for the junior Eagles,' I say, which is

true. Our team played a team from down Pemberton way.

'Did you win?' says Noah.

'Not then, but with my local team we did,' I say, 'We won a premiership.'

'Can I see the photos?' asks Noah. For some reason, today seems as good a time as any to go back to those memories. I go to my office, open the drawer I never usually open, and fish out the stack of photos held together by an elastic band.

I bring them to the kitchen table and Noah files through them. 'Who's that?'

'Rockwell! Top bloke. Really funny, you should hear him do horse races. You'd crack up, seriously.'

Noah laughs, although that's mostly because I'm laughing, and less because he knows what I'm on about. 'And this guy?'

'Streaks.'

'Who's "Streaks?"'

'He was a legend,' I say. 'The deepest voice. It used to make me laugh. He'd say, "Shut up, Rockwell!"'

'And you guys won the grand final?'

I nod. 'We did, although it wasn't really about that. It's the friendships; it doesn't matter if you haven't seen them for years, you're mates, and always will be.'

'Who's that?' says Noah. He points to a boy with blond hair, head high, and his hand on my left shoulder, a pat on the back as we head off the ground.

I pause. 'That's Jeremy. He was the captain.'

'Was he good?'

I smile. 'He was awesome.'

I've had many friends in my life. Why did Jeremy's loss cut so deep? That I can't say, although I also took the sudden death of a cousin earlier that decade, just as hard.

I think it's because we live under the illusion that we will always get enough time with those we love. We think there will always be the chance to say something we really want to say, or to hug someone or take their hand. And then they're gone, and we're struck with the reality of knowing we'll never get to see them again.

In revisiting my lost friendship with Jeremy, I see that what was once a space of guilt and regret has now moved to a place of acceptance. He will always be with me in some way, given we grew up together, and shared hopes and dreams. But our friendship is no longer just a dark chapter in my life. In fact, I see it now as quite the opposite. In our friendship, we found a space where we could be real, raw and vulnerable without fear of judgement. Our time as friends provided a sanctuary for two sensitive kids scared their fears might outrun their dreams. And, in those all too brief years, we found a place where someone saw us, liked us, and in us found a better, brighter future.

I always imagined we would share that future. Still, he was with me as I wrote my next chapter; on the day after his funeral, I sat down with my notebook, and wrote *things that make life worth living*, with Jeremy as the first entry, in case, over time, I forgot just how vital his presence was, and always would be in my life.

# Homecoming

Between September 2020 and January 2021, my father visits hospital four more times for heart attack, heart failure and arrythmia, although the specifics don't matter. It's like labelling the ocean's numerous predators: they can all kill you if fate's not on your side on a given day.

During that time, I'm barely keeping it together. I'm less of a dad and more of an armed guard, always on alert for the next threat, or call to action. There's not much my kids can do, it seems, that doesn't send me into a freak-out.

Noah comes on one occasion, this time to a different, newer hospital. It says something about the state of the last one that it's a nicer place to visit, even when covered with scaffolding.

Dad's already out of bed and reading a book when we arrive at the ward. Noah takes that as a cue, immediately jumps into his bed, and starts laughing. I take a picture, and another, a welcome moment of frivolity in a place that is usually solemn.

In those months, I ferry coffee, and endure difficult conversations in the hope I'm somehow paying Dad back for all those times he was there for me. I take Dad home on two more occasions after that first, initial discharge with this same mission in mind.

On the first trip to York, after a four-week hospital stay, I'm grateful but exhausted and too willing to drop him home. Upon the second discharge, I lecture him about the importance of changing his diet, tell him he doesn't care, an echo of an earlier time, and more of a distraction to avoid facing the complexity of life, and the inevitability of death.

Upon the third hospital discharge, I finally get things right, as this is sometimes how long it can take a son to learn. And, while I should have parked out front, and I'm worried the long walk is the last thing he needs right now, I'm kind to him in the car, and grateful for his presence. We take him, not to his home of more than a decade, but to a smaller shack on the other side of York, as Alice is making the move, and so Dad needs to find a new place. He's found it, funnily enough, thanks to mates Yvonne and Giles; Yvonne's now in a retirement home, and Giles has died, and so it made sense to let one of their oldest friends call it home in a challenging time. As for the place, well, I didn't get a great look at it on the drop-off that first time around. From what I could see, it seemed dinky but lovable. It was hard not to be won over once you saw Dad had placed a photo of Giles in prime position on the mantle: two old mates, catching up, one holding on, and one already gone but always remembered.

Between Dad's various stays in hospital, my world slowly returns to normal. There's time to ride bikes with Noah. We usher in the return of Daddy–Josh days spent scoffing muffins at play centres, with coffee for me and juice for him. We have time enough for an hour or so in front of the TV, with him sitting on my thigh, his tiny, chubby legs dangling either side.

I grow to fear my phone vibrating on the weekend, given that's always the time, it seems, for Dad to return to hospital. I return to my psychologist; I had taken a break from seeing him after Dad's first stay in hospital, mainly because we never knew when we might be needed to again be at the hospital. And then, as I'm ready to return to my psychologist, my dad is readmitted, a fourth time, to Hollywood Hospital. It's agreed that I won't take him back, to give me a break. It's Luke's turn to take the wheel, drive Dad safely home, and help him get settled.

Luke and I agree to take my Dad's first week at home in three-day shifts to save him from having to go into assisted care. Luke stays down after the drop-off, and apparently there's more kookiness to the new joint than I first realised. Luke explains it to me fairly simply, but none of it adds up. It sounds, if I'm being blunt, like my dad is living in some kind of crazy house.

'It's all good, bro, I'll come on Monday,' I say, worried that when I get there, I'll see a tent with one pole missing.

'We need some power boards!' says Luke.

'What, he doesn't have any?'

'No, there's heaps,' says Luke. 'A couple of them, though, they're not so great. They make a popping noise.'

'A *popping* noise?'

'All good, bro, see you then,' says Luke and hangs up the phone.

I pull up at Dad's place the next week and notice, within minutes, the house's many quirks. For starters, the front door is two doors. When one door opens you can barely get through, and once you do the screen slams like the door to a jail cell. As for the rest of the house? Well, it's different. There's a gap between where the walls end and the ceiling starts, the lights seem attached to what I can only describe as toilet plumbing, there is not a single light switch on the wall – they are all hidden in the doorframes or on top of cupboards, it's like a 'Choose your level of luminescence' adventure anytime you try to shed some light on proceedings.

Now and then a fat rat comes in and dies, spreadeagled, on the kitchen floor. If you're lucky you'll find a moth in your bed but, more likely, a spider. The shower door doesn't work. There's a record-player in case you missed Slim Dusty the first time around. None of the windows open. The bathroom is roughly the size of a shoebox.

Only, as I stand outside of it, I'm not struck by all that. I'm thinking of the kind, funny and generous man who once snapped a photo of me at Cafe Bugatti all those years back, passed away, and then, years later, even after his death, gave my dad a place to stay.

Luke's standing in the kitchen and he looks a little jumpy. He pulls me outside, lights a rollie, and takes a puff. 'Mate, I've done some shoddy gigs in my time, but I have never seen power boards this bad. You think you can replace them?'

'Sure.' I'm grateful to have something practical to do. While

I have always had a soft spot in my heart for York, it's never a good place in which to be bored. 'Anything else?'

'I don't think the cuckoo clock works. But if you want to,' says Luke, 'look it over, give it a tweak. And leave out some snacks for Dad, just nibblies and stuff.' I say I will, though I can't help thinking Dad's a person, not a cat.

Luke leaves, and it's just me and Dad. I know he's already over us being around so much, but also aware that someone will need to stay with him for this first week post-surgery. As people go, me and Luke aren't bad options. We're fairly casual and not particularly nagging. He can't drive straight away, though, not after the insertion of a new pacemaker, and so he's more reliant on us than he'd like.

We get through as best we can. I watch more news than I usually would (an old person's game, all that faith in traditional media channels). I cook him dinner, mostly omelettes, but I grab him some ready meals too, as I'm terrified he's not eating properly. I also replace those old power boards with surge control, next-level plug management. That's eight boards in total, and a fair whack of cash.

On day two, it's Dad's first outing since arriving home. I drive him to the Men's Shed in my white Elantra, now tinged with waves of red dirt sprayed up onto the sides.

Dad's quiet on the drive, but it's not a long one. We turn right, head towards the huge silver shed in the middle of the field. We stop alongside a haphazard row of cars. We walk up slowly to the shed and by the time we're near the door, my socks are covered in spikelets from the foxtail grass.

Dad tells me they'll be mid-meeting by this point of the morning. He also says he's not sure how long he'll be able to stay. I wonder if he says this to appease me, as it's not like I fell in love with the place the first time around. Or maybe these hospital stays have really knocked him around. He's not easy to read at the best of times. Since those stays, he's more jokey than usual, and for some reason that's more worrying than his typical balance of wit and candour.

I open a large metal door for Dad, peering in, and they look back at me, a collective, 'Who is that?' as they struggle to work out why I'm there or if they've ever seen me before.

Dad trails behind me. As he enters the shed, the president falls silent. Then in unison, the men applaud. I step aside to let Dad through as the men continue to applaud, and find myself tearing up from the show of respect.

I get another day or two with Dad, cooking brekky, replacing light bulbs, clearing cobwebs, and filling his fridge and freezer with the good stuff. He's mildly embarrassed by the whole palaver. I say, 'Too bad,' and make him promise to never again go back to hospital. He says he can't promise that, but it's worth me trying, all the same.

When it's time to go home, it's hard to leave him on his own. I struggle for a bit until he says, 'I'm fine, Laurie, for Christ's sake, I'm fine,' which breaks the tension.

I take my suitcase out to the car, he says, 'You did well, back there.'

'What, at the Men's Shed?'

'No, at the hospital,' he says. 'Awful place.'

'I was always going to get you out of there,' I say.

'You might not have had the choice,' he says, and leaves it at that. 'How's your writing going?'

'Yeah, not bad,' I say. 'I got a fellowship. Heading to the Blue Mountains.'

'You don't seem that excited.'

'No, it's just the collection, it hasn't exactly set the world on fire.'

'That's pretty much the artist's lot,' he says. 'Always was, always will be.'

I get to the car, load the suitcase in the boot. A brief embrace, ended sooner by Dad, as he's never been great with big Hollywood hugs.

'Be good to get some time to write,' I say.

'And dare I say it, some time to miss your lovely children,' he says, and laughs a wicked chuckle.

'My kids? Little angels,' I say. 'I mean, apart from the noise. And the spills. Oh, and the breakages.'

'Don't forget the bruises.'

'What, mine or theirs?' I say, and then sigh. 'I love you, Dad.'

'I love you too,' he says, his voice going high and distorted.

'You've got enough food?'

'Yep.'

'And the gardener's coming Friday.'

'You betcha.'

'And you sure you're going to be okay?'

'For Christ's sake, just go. Go!' he says, laughing, and walks inside.

# The Gift

I arrive at Varuna – The National Writers' House in Katoomba, in the Blue Mountains, New South Wales, in June 2021. It's busy at the airport but eerily quiet on public transport because of the pandemic. It's nine years since I first came here, but it feels like a lifetime ago. We had no kids at that point and had only recently married. So much, it seems, was still to come, although, at the time, I'd felt distinctly more a man of letters than nappies, bibs and onesies.

On the night before I fly out, I sneak first into my younger son's room, and then my elder's, and watch them sleep for a bit. In a film, it's a cliché when a mother or father pulls the blanket over their child. In our house, it's a necessity, as our youngest stretches horizontally across the head of the bed, his cheek smushed into the mattress. So I pull the blankets over him, knowing full well I will likely have to do it again later that night.

I call my friend Dash. He tells me that if I write nothing on this trip, it will still be an unforgettable part of my life: the time I went on a writing retreat, and no words came.

I thank him. He says, 'Man, you're welcome. Enjoy this, okay?' For the first time in a long time, we don't talk about the Philadelphia 76ers.

I go to bed. Wake up, thinking it's time to go at ten thirty. Wake up, thinking it's time to go at one am. Wake up one last time, sure it must be time to go at three am, and then nap fitfully until it's finally time to wake up and get ready for the flight.

On previous flights, I felt truly alone. These days, my phone, laptop, and iPad all have my sons' toothy grins as their screensaver. They say, 'we belong to you'. It's only now, at the thought of leaving Annaya and my boys, that I realise how inherently I belong to them as much, if not more, than to my life as a writer.

The taxi drops me at 141 Cascade Street, and I walk up the curved driveway of what was once the Dark family residence. Once the yellow house of renown comes into view, I get tingles all over my body. So many times, over so many years, I had wanted to return. Wishes aren't much if the world doesn't want it, though, and it was never the right time, not with Noah's needs and late-night wakes with Josh keeping me anchored in Western Australia.

Inside, the living room walls are lined with books from previous residents, with many whose names are held in reverence: Charlotte Wood, John Kinsella, Jessie Cole, Tegan Bennett Daylight.

During our welcome drinks, the CEO tells us selections here are based not on marketability or the commercial appeal of a book, but on literary merit. That's something I can appreciate and while my execution has at times been a little off, my motivation has always been to write something significant, rather than topical. In charting the universal, I have always aimed, or maybe dreamed, to be timeless rather than timely.

I'm here having won the 2021 Henry Handel Richardson Flagship Fellowship for short stories. The win is a vote of confidence for my short fiction, only that joy feels guarded by my inner critic, and held captive until the point that I've secured publication for the collection.

I meet Varuna's consultant, Elizabeth, on my second day in residence. She's tiny, fragile, her face taken up mostly by her smile. Speaks quietly, patiently, in a Canadian accent. Once we have sat down, I talk a lot about my literary world, my hopes, my dreams, and the fear that nothing's ever going to be the same now that I have kids.

I tell her I have two projects: one is a labour of love, forged from the fires of sixteen years writing short stories, and many more reading them, always obsessed with the idea that one day I might publish a short story collection of my own. I tell her it's stuck, and I don't know how to fix it, and put my face in my hands.

She looks at me. Waits, but I remain silent. 'And what about the other one?'

I laugh and tell her my boy wrote five words on my whiteboard, his way to help me step away from *Greater City Shadows*. I tell her I'm afraid to write outside of my genre, but excited by the opportunity to write in my own, less conditional voice.

I tell her I drafted ten thousand words on first the plane from Perth to Sydney, and on the train from Sydney to Katoomba. I tell her that on that train, there was a youngish guy named Jacob, who couldn't have been more than twenty-five. He lived in a tent he carried with him, told me darkness is sometimes more kind and more comforting than light, when you get used to it. That, as I got off at Katoomba, he paused, and then said, 'I think I'll get off at Katoomba too.'

I asked him where he was staying, and he said he didn't know. I asked which way I should go out of the station, and he said, 'You'll know when we get there.' That he blocked me, arms out, body rigid, and still smiling, when I tried to walk in the wrong direction.

I said, 'What are you doing?'

He said, 'I'm stopping you from going the wrong way.'

She laughs. 'That's quite the story.' She pauses, smiles. Says, 'So, what are you waiting for?'

'You mean I don't have to work on *Greater City Shadows*?'

'You don't *have* to do anything,' she says, and I laugh.

'So I can write the memoir?'

'Yes.'

'Can you give me permission? I know it's silly, but can you do that?'

She puts her palms together, leans forward, and says, 'I give you permission. Now, go! Go write your next book.'

That night, Kate, who is a fellow resident, asks me what I think of Tim Winton. I pass off a couple of generic points about this writer whose male characters I had studied in such depth. I think, *I hate him. I love him. I mean, it's complicated.*

'You?'

'I think he's wonderful,' she says. 'The work, it's wonderful,' and I know that's the truest of the thoughts. That, on some level, it's hard not to be inspired by his words and the way they linger on the Australian literary landscape.

'You ever met him?'

'What, Tim Winton?'

She nods.

'No,' I say. 'But it often feels like he is there, his words forever circling around my state, and my city.'

I don't say that last part. I've felt it before, though, and sometimes feel it still. But if I never turn out to be a literary giant, I will still, like everyone who has visited Varuna, be a writer and significant part of the house, and its shared history.

My coach, Marie, has made me a self-compassion guided meditation for the trip, and I listen to it every night. It's seriously the best thing I have heard in my life, like a spoken word performance, only this one targets certain thoughts each time I listen to it.

The idea, I guess, is to cut off my anxiety at the pass, never letting my fears of failure gather too much velocity while I'm trying to create new work. Additionally, my (relatively) new psych works on creating a group of 'resources' for me, meant for another run of upcoming EMDR sessions, but also applicable in a high intensity and hopefully high productivity time such as this.

Without telling you too much, or giving away the wonders of psychology, each person in my resources sits or stands in an imagined clearing in my mind. It's a fine, warm night, and there's a campfire, and some logs surrounding the campfire. The people in my resources are there to guide me, answer questions, or, in the case of my compassion, to wrap me up in a massive hug and talk sweetly to me until the demons have dissipated enough, and my fears have been chased away.

By the end of the fortnight in Varuna, I've drafted 77,500 words at 5,000 words a day, after my starting count of 12,500 from the plane and train trips. I think of my three unpublished novel manuscripts. Of the two hundred plus short stories forged, and mostly forgotten, aside from those few that worked out the way I wanted them to.

I also think about the friendships I've just made, and how none of them required me to 'do' anything. I just had to be me, and that was enough.

Are you there?

*I'm here.*

What did you want for me?

*A future*, says the inner critic. *Only I knew you couldn't see it, and I was worried you'd be lost, paralysed by fear. So instead, I told you the truth. That from here, it was up to you. That you needed to survive.*

Haven't we done that?

*Do you still get scared sometimes?*

Of course. That's life, though. I mean it's lonely when it's just me, you know? There's so much pressure in that space, and so much I don't yet know.

*I'm here.*

But you're always freaking out. I mean fuck, maybe once, you could say *nailed it* or *great job*, just to break up the pattern. Why can't you just let me be me?

*I know it was hard, and I know it was lonely. But you did it, just now, and can you see? From here on, it's just you, and you've got this, I promise. You can count on me if you need me, unless you hate me, and I wouldn't blame you if you hate me. But I don't hate you; I love you, and I was only trying to help.*

On my last day I catch the train early from Katoomba back to Sydney. There's no Jacob this time, only people on their way to work. I have arranged to meet Lindy, a friend and short-story writer, in Sydney's CBD for a quick breakfast.

We eat breakfast – my only truly decadent breakfast for the trip – a cheese and egg brioche burger, minus the bacon, like a Big Mac if it got into macro nutrients. She tells me about K-Drama, and I tell her about C-Pop, and the song 'Red Sun', that took me out of the shadows and again allowed me to be me, for all the ups and down that it brings.

'It's good to see you again,' she says. I wonder when she has ever seen me, and then remember that in all those years of tackling narrative arcs, scaling structure and emotional deep-dives under the guise of short fiction, we've done this before, years earlier.

A drive around Sydney after a celebratory dinner for a recently released short story anthology. She pulled us out of a too-tight parking spot on Norton Street and said, 'I want to show you my city.' It felt somewhat strange, kind and of wondrous because every story I'd written was me saying those same words, over and over.

We got lost, although eventually we found the Harbour Bridge, and in time we made our way to Gelato Messina. They all manner of flavours at the front counter – from bounty to blood orange, to *dulce de leche* – all glowing under warm, bright lights. all glowing under warm, bright lights. 'We ordered sweet treats and then wandered the streets of Newtown. I shared my take on the craft, and she shared hers, and it was all a bit surreal but incredibly grounding to talk short stories with someone who loved them just as much as me.

On the drive home, I spotted a CD cover on the floor of the passenger side. Four Shaun Micallefs standing together in navy-blue jackets, next to three yellow wheelie bins. A lost classic at track five, the aptly named 'Christopher Walken Sings David Bowie (Fashion)'.

'Holy shit, you own this?'

'Yeah!' says Lindy. 'I love it.'

'Oh my God, can we please put this on?

We play it, track five on repeat, and drive around the city streets, writers forever seeking perfection, insight, and flawlessness on the page, enraptured by how silly and exquisite a song can be when it no longer has to be perfect.

# Inheritance

There are more lockdowns throughout 2021. We return to afternoon baths, play kid Cluedo (there's one franchise I never expected to branch out into a junior version) and 'cook' brownies, mostly from the packet to the point that our baking trays build a crumb-stubble on their edges.

All the while, the world remains off-kilter. On the other side of the country, COVID numbers skyrocket. I speak to writers on sketchy Zoom connections and remind them how much their words matter. I tell them to be brave and remind them they never know how close they are to their next big opportunity.

As that happens, my anxiety maintains its steady litany: Mum will get sick again, and Dad will end up back in hospital; a publisher will tell me they hated Greater City Shadows so much they set the manuscript on fire.

Still, in recent times the anxiety has been joined by another steady voice: a voice of gratitude and the sense that things in my life – give or take a crisis – are actually pretty good. That for now, all is love, joy and abundance. For every anxious thought, a calmer, kinder thought often reminds me that things have turned out okay. For each time I've feared the worst, what actually arrived, while difficult, was never a full-blown catastrophe.

That's not to say the worst won't someday arrive in my life.

It's more that when it does, I'll deal with it then, knowing I can handle it, and that, if I really can't, there will be enough people around to help me, and ways in which to remember to stay grateful.

This hits home most profoundly on a quiet Sunday morning, with the chance to go see Dad at somewhere other than a hospital. He's still in his new place in York, his wheatbelt town in Western Australia, two hours out of Perth. It's still tiny, still boxy, and hot, like a gardener's shed, though it kind of suits the new, resourceful and resilient Dad. If he's not choosing his rocks for the next town fair, he's sitting atop his Lawn Boss, a green-and-gold ride-on lawnmower with more juice than my Elantra could ever possibly muster.

We leave Perth at nine thirty. Josh and Noah do not travel well this trip, or indeed on any trip. They start asking if we're there the moment we turn onto the freeway. The only way to placate them is to play a song that Josh likes, and one that Noah likes, and these likes are in no way compatible, more ways to start a fight, than tunes to guide us there.

Josh starts singing. Noah complains. 'It's my song,' he says. 'He can't sing on my song.'

'I like the song,' says Josh, and sings louder.

Noah does this thing where he's talking normally at first but then as he getsstressedouthestartssayingthingsincredibly-loudlyandincrediblyquickly. Annaya threatens to turn off the music, and they quiet down.

What types of songs do they play? 'We Go Together', not from Grease, but from *The Secret Life of Pets*. A cover of

'I Like to Move It' when I didn't much like the original version. 'All I Want for Christmas is You', which is a good song … at Christmas. And then, as I'm already struggling, 'Happy' by Pharrell Williams comes along, and is as welcome as a fart in a buffet line.

Still, we're not done. As we hit the outer north-eastern locality of The Lakes, thirty minutes or so out of York, Noah requests 'Raining Tacos', which is not only shit, but which lifts the melody from 'Pachelbel's Canon'. This means an all-time classic, speculated to have been written as a gift to Bach's brother who was about to be wed, is now a fuck-you ear worm dedicated to the combination of corn chip, mince, and lettuce. It's the pits, and yet I always feel *something* when I hear it, a deep longing melancholy, which is probably what Pachelbel intended when he omitted all mention of sour cream, cheese or any other condiments from his original version.

My enjoyment of novelty tracks has plummeted since becoming a parent because that's mostly what kids listen to, and because these songs sucked then, and they suck now. More recently, though, it feels as if these songs have mutated, and found new levels of annoying in their choices of words, styles, and instrument. 'Raining Tacos' is the end boss of such songs, its incessant bass-beat matched only by my own increased heartbeat.

But it's not just the song that's getting to me. People talk about life-changing events all the time, but they rarely talk about the days that follow, when you try to make sense of it all, but still feel fundamentally out of whack. Maybe it's shock, or maybe PTSD. I'm not sure it matters; all I know is that despite my determination to get on with things, I'm still processing all that's happened since my Dad fell off a roof, and into a coma.

We drive on, thankfully moving from 'Raining Tacos' to OneRepublic, 'Counting Stars', and Noah's really feeling the latter, he always does, so I sing along too, the closest we'll get today to musical synergy. I want to tell him about the time my dad nearly died after falling off a roof. How I felt different afterwards and was worried I would not be able to be the dad I needed to be. How that day, when I first heard Noah's gurgled cry, I thought, *I will do all I can to get things right as a father.*

I want to tell my boy that I never, ever, don't love him. That each time I slip up, or get short with him, it's only because I'm afraid of the role entrusted to me. That I find him challenging, of course, but necessarily so, and even so I'm still afraid, and I feel small, a speck of dust looking after a gemstone.

Instead, I sing along with him because this is about Noah, not me, and I feel that my voice, shouting out in chorus with him, is more likely what he wants more than anything else.

When we arrive at York, Dad hands me a crate. It contains my letters to him, more than twenty-five years of correspondence, my manuscripts I've sent him over the years, and my first published articles, stories and poems. There are some photos of people my dad used to know, and I wonder if, in some roundabout way, he's saying, Please, just help me let go.

We head to lunch, at a serviceable café. The café we've found is very York, by which I mean it's next door to an old building, and has three tables full of locals talking shop.

We order inside, take a table up on the patio, order foods we know the kids won't likely eat. The boys run off almost immediately to the playground. I go to follow, but Annaya pats my arm, stands up and wanders over to join them.

'It's good to be here with you, Dad.'

'I know, it was a close one. I came perilously close to death.'

'But we got you home.'

'You got me home,' he says.

Again, it's burgers for lunch, an ongoing challenge to mortality, it seems, since Dad's was first brought into question. I eat mine slowly, with silly thoughts popping up. I worry about Dad choking on some bun; the patio floor caving in, or the roof falling down. And then I see everything's changed.

And then I see a greater, more pressing concern. Each time I see Dad might be the last time I see him.

'How's your lunch?' says Dad.

'It's good,' I say. 'I mean, the lettuce is a bit droopy, and the tomato—' I catch myself, take a breath. 'I mean, it's good,' I say. 'A perfectly decent burger.'

We eat our food quietly, although the serenity is occasionally broken up by the hurricane swoosh of Noah as he speeds in, takes a bite of his burger, and runs off again, a baseball-capped whirlwind, in and then out of the scene. Josh is a little slower and shorter, so it's his red fisherman's hat we see first, bobbing above the tabletop, and then his hand, reaching up and grabbing a fistful of chips.

Soon enough it's time to finish up with both our lunch and our visit to York. We'd like to stay longer but it's a two-hour drive home, so we take our time together where we can get it, and hope it is enough.

'Wait. Photo op.'

'Nah,' says Dad, pushing at me with his arm.

'Please?' And then he sees all that's underlying my request for a picture: what we've been through these past months, all that fear that we might never reach the days we'd so relied upon to help counterbalance, our ups, our downs, and in-betweens.

He poses. He laughs. He pulls one of those faces dads pull when they're trying to be silly. He laughs again, pulls another silly face, and then finally rests into a smile, and I leave the phone up, staring at that smile, pretending there's a shot or two more to go, when really, I'm done.

'You got it?'

'I got it.'

We walk out into a scorching day in York and on to our cars. We take some family photos this time, all of us in sunnies except for Noah, who stares out stoic from beneath his cap. Then Dad comes into the pics, Annaya is happy to take over. Dad's smiling, joking around, and almost immediately, Noah starts smiling too, gazing up at his grandfather in pure joy. I'm in the middle, smiling obliviously, missing things, as I sometimes do.

With pictures taken, I hug my dad. I pat his back, mapping the feeling until the next time, while my boys grab his legs, and hug him too.

'See you soon,' says Dad, and hops into his SUV, a black subcompact, with dirt skating up the wheelhouse. He backs out, and then drives off, a chorus of 'I love you!' from the boys, Annaya and me.

On the drive home, I say, 'Noah, do you want to play "Red Sun?"' but he shakes his head, and asks for 'Raining Tacos'. The moment it hits, Josh slots on his bright green headphones to protect him from the incoming aural barrage.

The song is godawful, the worst. And yet, there's something about it that gets to me, and likely always will.

I start to cry, not from the music, or maybe it is, and it's complicated, how a song detailing a storm of Mexican cuisine, passed on without any believable context, can still fill me with emotion.

I want to stop the song, and I want to play the song because I know it's in these waves of emotion that I'll start to feel better. I know that in his love of raining tacos, Noah's reaching out in the only way he knows, and that if I reach back, and feel what I need to feel, then we'll be okay.

And I hate this song so much, and it's hard driving away from a home not grounded by place but by a person. I hope one day I can be that much of a home for my boys. That I can survive raining tacos, familial flaws, and my fears that I won't become even half the dad my father turned out to be.

We speed along the Great Southern Highway, twists and turns, and golden fields, cropped wheat, left and right. In an act of desperation, and to break this spell of C-Pop, Annaya lifts off Josh's headphones, says, 'Hey baby, you want to listen to something?'

Josh nods and says, '"Peace Like a River".' Annaya quickly finds the song – anything to stop the culinary downpour – presses play, and I'm happy and sad, all at once, with a kinder, calmer voice to guide me home.

We drive on in silence, hurtling home, sunbeams scattered through the trees.

# ACCEPTING

What's it like to be an anxious father?

Well, I'm always ready to spring into action. This means I clocked the shadow gliding along the ocean floor seconds prior to the gasps of other swimmers and have already shouted 'Stingray!' before rushing my kids to safety. It means that no emotion they have, however small it might seem to another fully grown adult, is ever diminished, discouraged or ridiculed.

Sometimes this saves my kids from injury or embarrassment. At other times, they're saved only from the ghosts that rattle around my head, or my fears around fate, or the thought of losing them. And sometimes I realise, belatedly, that they never needed saving in the first place.

For better or worse, anxiety is a part of my brain's operating system. I control its effects mostly by eliminating old or outdated commands. Self-care – in my case, ongoing therapy, writing, regular exercise, and connection with like-minded friends and fellow writers – helps overwrite what were once undeniable prompts towards denial, detachment and isolation. Anxiety kicks in most often for me when I'm thinking rather than doing; it whispers when I'm alone in a darkened room. It tends to dissipate when I'm chowing down on a kick-arse brekkie with a friend, a special celebratory episode of the Mish and Loz Show, where the hours pass like minutes and the only thing I worry about is glancing at my watch and seeing, sadly, that again it's time to go.

At home, my mental heavy lifting takes its toll. It's hard to know what to share with my boys in relation to that subject. In such situations, Annaya often passes on the news: *Dad needs a break, kids. He's struggling, he needs five minutes.* And I think it's good for kids to hear that too.

So, what are the things that have helped tip the scales in favour of this anxious, loving father?

When I'm in desperate need of a break, I take it, if it's possible to do so. I've learned the hard way that carrying on is much more likely to do damage than a much-needed timeout, so I've had to learn greater self-care, and increase awareness of when I'm heightened to the point that I'm beginning to shut down.

When I feel isolated or alone, I pick up the phone, and don't start scrolling, but use it like a phone. I call a friend and say hi. Or I reach out to mates from further back where the times were mostly good but we drifted apart. With them, I can recall the songs and the sounds of who we were; the crushes and the characters; first concerts and school balls; shaky hand-cam footage from the last days of year twelve, and a yearbook covered in messages.

When I feel lost, I set one or two manageable goals that will bring me happiness. I listen to an Eluvium album, watch *I'm Alan Partridge* if I need a chuckle, or hit up any one of the talks from Jack Kornfield's time teaching at Spirit Rock. I revisit films I first watched at the cinema. And man, *Run Lola*

*Run* was the shit, you know? So fun, and fresh and different, and even now it's cool to imagine your life unravel in three different ways, all dependent on what you choose to do at a particular point.

Instead of putting it on my partner, I check in regularly with myself to see how I'm travelling, emotionally and spiritually, and note the response that comes back: where I'm rocking it, the ways in which I am struggling, and how things could feel better rather than worse. The answers I receive sometimes surprise me and can at times feel a little confronting. They also provide the opportunity for me to tweak things, or create change, and I need that as part of creating and recreating a soulful, purposeful life.

This is what I've learned as I have moved from being Laurie the single guy to Laurie the man with a family: that as a parent, I am still entitled to my feelings, needs and desires. And ultimately, that helps me to be part of a connected, loving family. By extension, every member of that unit has that same right to support, companionship or time alone. Our parenting pact, when applied and remembered (and remembering can be hard with so much stuff going on) is that we have each other's backs, putting our kids necessarily first, but also knowing when we need help, and being able to ask for it.

It's a simple concept. It also takes much work on both our parts to make it a reality. But it is work that we love, and work we're willing to do.

My own nuclear family is one of many types of families in society. In my world and, I hope, in the real world, our merit as caregivers can be judged, first and foremost, in relation to the love we give, and the ways in which we continue to support, nurture and encourage our children as they grow into kind, compassionate adults. It's not surprising, then, that I often empathise with parents I see out in the world. It would be strange to tell you this each time I'm standing alongside you in a playground or sitting nearby at a local café. It might be off-putting for me to go, 'Aw!' whenever I see a child light up as a dad goes for a tickle, or a mum nuzzles into her bub's cherubic face, their noses squidged together like two lumps of Play-Doh. I feel these moments deeply, though, and see in each the language we all share, forever hoping that we are doing okay at the demanding, seemingly unending job of being a loving, present parent.

I love my kids. I bet you love yours too; that you go above and beyond because they echo in your heart. A gentle thump, it almost feels, alongside yours, as you go about your day.

And I bet your kids love you just as much. That you're their sun and moon; the clouds in the sky, the breeze that cools their skin on a hot afternoon. I bet that just by being you, you make their world a kinder, safer place.

That's what a kid needs more than anything else. They need you there, flaws and all, as you both try to make sense of the world. They need an alchemy of things which they don't yet know or understand. An opportunity to turn their fears into futures. Someone to tell them, 'You mean everything to me.'

# Acknowledgements

This book was drafted in Katoomba, on the lands of the Gundungurra and Darug people, and completed in Boorloo (Perth), on Whadjuk Noongar Boodjar. I pay my respects and thanks to the traditional custodians of the land and their elders, past, present and emerging.

Many of the names of the people who appear in this book have been changed to protect their anonymity. Those names that remained unchanged were included either to give necessary context on Australia's literary landscape at the time of my debut novel's publication or to acknowledge the inspiration provided by literary and musical forbears as I found my own style, voice, and way of engaging with the world.

My heartfelt thanks to my publisher and editor, Georgia Richter, who worked tirelessly and patiently with me on this project and encouraged me to write with necessary vulnerability and authenticity. Thanks also to fellow Fremantle Press editor Kirsty Horton, who spotted inconsistencies in early versions of the manuscript and opened up necessary avenues of discussion in relation to parenting. Thanks to Claire Miller and Chloe Walton for their enthusiasm, professionalism and good humour, Fremantle Press CEO Alex Allan, and former CEO Jane Fraser, who made me feel a part of the Fremantle

Press family long before my book was accepted for publication.

The WA literary community is a wonderfully welcoming place, with many people whom I've come to see as family. Thanks to Caroline, John, Sisonke, Logan, Claudia and all at the Centre for Stories for their support of this project, and for much needed and appreciated time and space to work on the book. Thanks also to Sharon Flindell, who championed our unique literary culture and helped adopt a greater, more inclusive and collaborative approach to the sector during her time at WritingWA.

Thanks to my fellow writers and students from the west who've offered friendship and support: Brooke Dunnell, Nathan Hobby, David Allan-Petale, Mel Hall, Brody Stevens, Melinda Tognini, Susan Midalia, Brigid Lowry, Amanda Curtin, Josephine Clarke, Rashida Murphy, Heather Delfs, Amanda Kendle, Kyra Giorgi, Zoe Deleuil, Hannah Van Didden, Emily Paull, Holden Sheppard, Raphael Farmer, Esme Wilmot, Emma Young, Josh Langley, Belinda Hermawan, and all the members, past and present, of The Subcommittee. Thanks to Mark Keenan, who reminded me what I was writing about, who for, and why it mattered. Thanks to Rebecca Laffar-Smith, who knew exactly what to say, and in the process opened me to greater kindness and self-compassion. My enduring thanks to (relatively) east-coast friends and Laurie advocates Kate Larsen, Jo McClelland-Phillips, Jodi Cleghorn, Bel Woods, Sam Van Zweden, Ryan O'Neill, Les Zigomanis, Sue Robertson, Penny Gibson and Janey Runci.

Thanks to Jon Kraybill, Simon Miskin, Matthew McKeown, Alex Mcintosh, Marlo Rae, Alen Perich, Taylah Strano, Tristan Stein, Val Shay, Avantika Mehta, Rebecca Atkinson, Siobhan Lynch, Kristian Dawson, Justin Yukich and Isobella Clarke. Thanks to Jenny and Mark, Helen and Libby, Hollie and Dan, and Ingrid and Craig, who make me laugh, feed my soul, keep me sane, or give me some small sense of the world that lies outside of the written word. *Love, Dad* also honours the memory of Ricardo 'Rico' Capuano (1971–2022). He made the world a better place, he will be missed, and I'm forever grateful for his friendship and generosity.

I wrote this book with generous support from the Australia Council for the Arts, the Department of Local Government, Sport and Cultural Industries, Varuna – The National Writers' House, Minderoo Foundation, and Forrest Research Foundation. Versions of two chapters of this book were previously published online: 'Safety and Security' was published as 'The Mountains' in Issue Three of *Portside Review*, and 'Like Riding a Bike' was published in *Journal*, both produced by the Centre for Stories and edited by Robert Wood, whose early support was integral to the book's development. Time under the tutelage of Rebecca Giggs at Faber Writing Academy proved similarly pivotal. Thanks to Rebecca and Academy Manager Sam Twyford-Moore for their industry insight, generosity and ongoing support for both this project and those yet to come.

My book was also supported by some particularly innovative thinkers in and outside of the literary sector. Special thanks to

Che, Paul, Steven and David, Clare Goodall Travis, Dr Chau Nguyen, Richard Keeler, Ella McNeill, Helen Mathie, Virginia Mosk, James Arvanitakis, Paul Johnson, my fellow writers at Varuna and Faber Writing Academy in 2021, the members of the 2022 Cohort of the Minderoo Foundation Artist Fund, and to Barry McGuire, who welcomed me in with a single smile and the words, warmth, and wisdom that followed.

Thanks to my mother, my father, my brothers and my sister. I love you, and I'm grateful for all you did to instill in me a sense of humour, a love of storytelling and a greater understanding of family. Thanks to Annaya's family for love and support in good times and challenging.

Finally, thanks to my wife and two beautiful boys, to whom this book is dedicated, and who fill me with hope, joy and wonder. You are everything to me and I'm honoured to be part of our open, loving, imperfect family.

## ALSO AVAILABLE

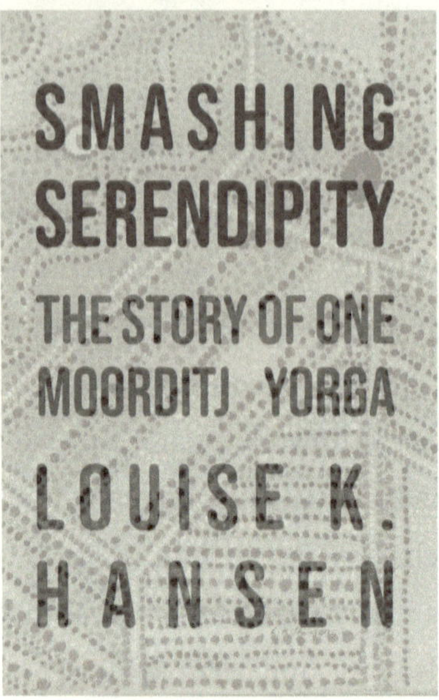


Lavinia Connell grows up in a small town where racist attitudes and violence against Aboriginal people occur every day. Her parents ensure her family stays together, while other cousins and friends are removed by the state. Violence and adversity occur time and again, even while Lavinia excels at sport and at school, drawing on her own inner strength and physical resourcefulness. In time, Lavinia will find herself a homeless young widow with four young children. But she uses education and determination to bring her small family back together, and finds love when she least expects it.

*'This poignant memoir is a reminder that there are generations of Aboriginal women who, in addition to experiencing trauma and pain at the hands of settlers, also have stories of perseverance and strength.'*
Books + Publishing

First published 2023 by
FREMANTLE PRESS

Fremantle Press Inc. trading as Fremantle Press
PO Box 158, North Fremantle, Western Australia, 6159
fremantlepress.com.au



Cover photograph by shutterstock.com/GoodStudio; shutterstock.com/Shtonado
Designed by Carolyn Brown, tendeersigh.com.au

A catalogue record for this book is available from the National Library of Australia

ISBN 9781760992064 (paperback)
ISBN 9781760992071 (ebook)

Fremantle Press is supported by the Western Australian State Government through the Department of Cultural Industries, Tourism and Sport.

Fremantle Press respectfully acknowledges the Whadjuk people of the Noongar nation as the Traditional Owners and Custodians of the land where we work in Walyalup.

www.ingramcontent.com/pod-product-compliance
Lightning Source LLC
LaVergne TN
LVHW091113080826
845145LV00008B/1896

* 9 7 8 1 7 6 0 9 9 2 0 6 4 *